FRAN,

I ENJOYED STUDYING WITH YOU AT
WESTERN. EQUIP THE SAINTS . . .

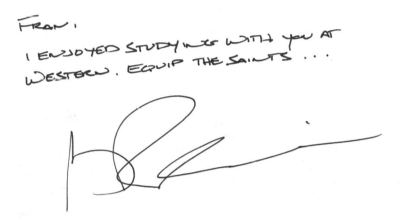

Endorsements

Dr. David Hesselgrave
Professor Emeritus of Missions, Trinity Evangelical Divinity School

"Over long years I have increasingly felt that the crying need of the STM (Short-Term Missions) movement is to be rooted in a long-term field-based strategy. Provided that STM volunteers are committed to Christ and prepared to communicate the biblical gospel, that crying need can be met by establishing strategic partnerships with the on-going ministries of like-minded churches and missions in targeted areas. George Robinson does an outstanding job of demonstrating how the strategic use of STM can be met and managed. Absolutely no book with which I am acquainted does a better job of addressing this need both theoretically and practically than does *Striking the Match*. He is to be congratulated for this accomplishment and the book is to be commended to churches, missions and schools. You really can't afford to undertake a short-term mission until you have studied it!"

Dr. George Patterson
Author of *The Church Multiplication Guide* and
Adjunct Missions Professor, Western Seminary

"George Robinson has a habit that disturbs some people--he thinks! His passion for discovering truths not only in God's Word but also in God's work has led to disciplined, objective research and yielded his practical, to-the-point, instruction. His experience overseas, academic training and writing skills combine to help Christian workers strike that match that taps God's power to ignite a church planting movement. I have found his insights and guidelines helpful as I mentored leaders aiming to help churches multiply in the New Testament way. My prayer is that you, too, will discover these treasures in *Striking the Match*."

Dr. Danny Akin
President, Southeastern Baptist Theological Seminary

"Our God is a missionary God, and He calls every Christ-follower to be engaged in fulfilling the Great Commission. *Striking the Match* provides a strategy showing how short-term missions (STM) can compliment and support long-term missions (LTM). The two can and should work together. George Robinson writes out of biblical conviction and first-hand experience from both sides of this partnership. You will be encouraged and excited by what you discover in these pages."

Dr. Enoch Wan
Doctor of Missiology Director, Western Seminary

"There is no lack of publication on the topic of STM in recent years. However, *Striking the Match* is unique in that it is based upon scholarly research that focuses on the quantitative and qualitative impact on the nationals hosting STM teams. Throughout the process of research and writing, I personally witnessed the author's commitment to academic excellence and methodological integrity. *Striking the Match* should be taken into consideration by missiologists, field missionaries, STM practitioners and North American church leaders who take seriously the desire to be strategic with all of the resources God has provided in the completion of the Great Commission."

Curtis Sargeant
Director of Int'l Church Planting, Saddleback Valley Community Church

"This account of how God is using lay people around the world to advance His Kingdom is both challenging and encouraging. e3 Partners is among those organizations that continue to adapt and grow as they watch for the Holy Spirit and seek to disciple the nations."

Paul Borthwick
Author, *How to Become a World Class Christian*
Senior Consultant, Development Associates International

"Unlike most of the resources which address short-term missions as stand-alone experiences, George Robinson presents how to strategically utilize this trend as a part of an overall, long-term strategy for expansion of the Kingdom of Christ. Read this book if you're interested in maximizing the long-term impact of your short-term missions efforts."

Dr. Gerald Harris
Editor, *The Christian Index* of the GA Baptist Convention

"George Robinson's book *Striking the Match* is a thorough and thought provoking work on how to maximize the effectiveness of short-term mission trips. He contends that STM teams can be incredibly significant in evangelizing the lost, helping to equip nationals and planting churches. In fact, this book emphasizes the importance of establishing reproducing indigenous churches using STM teams as catalysts in the process. His work is Biblically-based and well researched, yet extremely practical and readable. The book is a must read for any pastor or church interested in really making an eternal impact with their short-term mission teams."

Dr. Bruce Ashford
Professor of Missions, Southeastern Baptist Theological Seminary
Director of the Center for Great Commission Studies

"*Striking the Match* stands head-and-shoulders above other books charting a course for strategic short-term missions. It is grounded in biblical theology, sharpened by quantitative research, and seasoned by field experience. This is the book to read on short-term missions."

Dr. Sadiria Joy B. Tira
International Director, Filipino International Network and Senior Associate for Diaspora Studies of the Lausanne Committee for World Evangelization

"*Striking the Match* provides a significant positive contribution to the on-going debate regarding the validity of short-term mission. As an Asian church planter I enthusiastically recommend Dr. Robinson's work to both researchers and practitioners who desire to see the whole Church in the power of the Holy Spirit working to complete the Great Commission."

Carol Davis
Missions Consultant, LeafLine Initiatives

"If you are one that questions the value of short-term teams your view will radically adjust as you read *Striking the Match*. Be prepared for your heart to ignite, your vision to explode, and your prayers to deepen. Embracing the lessons from the models and principles cited in this book will grow us all. You too can strike that strategic match - as you join God in your distinctive place in Kingdom history."

Foreword

"Dr. George Robinson aptly describes the purpose and documents the impact of the e3 Mission experience. In the research behind this book, George validated the strengths and impact of our short term mission (STM) deployment for church planting. He confirmed that which we intuitively knew, or hoped, by observation for twenty years. He also identified several key improvements suggested by our national partners, particularly in the area of strengthening discipleship training and resources. Both the confirmation of the positive impact of e3 STM for church planting and the honest assessment of its inherent weaknesses are helping our ministry to improve. Likewise, I believe this book will serve others well to learn how to better mobilize this incredible resource available to us all - The Body of Christ - for the advancement of building up and multiplying churches.

The enterprise of world evangelization is too big, the need too urgent and the opportunity too great to persist in our thinking that the professional clergy or missionary is going to get the job done, apart from mobilizing a vast army of laymen and women to be "witnesses...to the very ends of the earth." The Biblical mandate is clear, to "equip the saints for the work of the ministry". Our heartbeat is to equip, mobilize and empower ordinary believers - goers, senders and receivers alike - to partner together in this "mission interdependence" to ignite church planting movements. Today e3 Partners fuels what it has helped to ignite by providing the tools and training needed by our national partners. They now take what they have learned from the e3 Mission model far beyond anything we could ever accomplish with North American mobilization alone, resulting in exponential growth of results on the field.

But, at the heart of it all is the conviction that our extraordinary God can accomplish extraordinary results with one ordinary layman who is trained to effectively present the Gospel, in partnership with an ordinary believer equipped and positioned to follow up for discipleship - all as part of a strategic long-term church planting movement. George Robinson shows us how to strike that match which the Holy Spirit is transforming into a great irresistible force of church planting for world evangelization.

Curtis V. Hail
President, e3 Partners

Striking the Match

George G. Robinson

e3 Resources
Franklin, Tennessee, U.S.A.

**Striking the Match
How God is Using Ordinary People to Change the World through Short-Term Missions**
Published and Distributed by e3 Resources,
317 Main Street Suite 207
Franklin, TN 37064

w w w . e 3 r e s o u r c e s . o r g

---

e3 Resources is a non-profit ministry based in Franklin, TN. Our mission is to develop innovative tools for the Body of Christ to use in effectively implementing their prayer, evangelism, and discipleship strategies for the glory of God. e3 Resources is a division of e3 Partners, based in Dallas, TX.

For other e3 Resources products please call your Christian supplier or contact us at: **888-354-9411** or **www.e3resources.org**.

Scripture taken from the HOLY BIBLE, NEW INTERNATIONAL VERSION®. NIV®. Copyright© 1973, 1978, 1984 by International Bible Society. Used by permission of Zondervan. All rights reserved.

The Holy Bible, English Standard Version® Copyright © 2001 by Crossway Bibles, a division of Good News Publishers. All rights reserved. Used by permission.

Library of Congress Cataloging-in-Publication Data
Robinson, George G. 1969-
Striking the Match: How God is Using Ordinary People to Change the World through Short-Term Missions/ Dr. George G. Robinson.
p. cm.
ISBN-10: 1-933383-37-8 (trade paperback)
ISBN-13: 978-1-933383-37-8 (trade paperback)
1. Missions. 2. Evangelism. 3. Church Planting.
I. Title.
2007943027

Printed in the United States of America

Contents

List of Abbreviations

CP   Church Planting

CPM   Church Planting Movement

LDC   Leadership Development Conference

LTM   Long–Term Missions

ND   National Director

POF   Professions of Faith

STM   Short–Term Missions

Acknowledgments

I wanted to thank the multitude of people whom God has used to shape my life and lead me deeper into His purposes. To name just a few:

To my beautiful bride Catherine, you are the most amazing woman that I have ever known. You are my best friend, my helpmate, and the one that makes life fun. Thank you for following me to the ends of the earth and back again and giving me three amazing little Robinsons along the way.

Mom, thank you for teaching me to keep moving forward and for always seeing more in me than I saw in myself.

Thanks to our incredible ministry partners and friends that not only have given so generously, but have under girded our family with prayer and encouragement as we work together in this sacred task.

Thanks also to those who contributed to my research directly: *Dr. Enoch Wan, Dr. Jerry Wofford, Curtis Hail, Mike Jorgensen, Mike Congrove, Todd Szalkowski*, and the hundreds of national brothers and sisters in over a dozen countries who have allowed us the privilege of serving them in mission as they seek to establish churches in their land and beyond.

This book is dedicated *to my "Naomi", Susan Dearie Jourdan*. As my mother-in-law, Susan gave me the most precious gift that I've received in this life following my salvation – her daughter. Susan went to be with Jesus while I was conducting the research that led to this book, but God used her courage and simple faith to bring out the "Boaz" in me.

Introduction

In 1996 God took a high school history teacher from Georgia who was a relatively new follower of Jesus and started him on an amazing adventure of discovery and spiritual growth. It was summer break and his wedding was only a few weeks away, but that teacher was faced with a Divine opportunity in response to the prayers of a woman whom at that time he had never met.

The woman's name was Itzel, and she lived in a fairly remote village in the Western part of Panama. Itzel, like so many people around the world, did not live within walking distance of a local church. She had become a Christian some time earlier and had been traveling quite a distance by bus each Sunday to worship in the nearest big city. Somewhere along the way Itzel came across the words of Jesus in Matthew 9:38 that tell us to "Ask the Lord of the harvest, therefore, to send out workers into his harvest field." So Itzel started praying for her small village that God would send someone to help her share the gospel with her neighbors and possibly even start a church right there in their midst.

That spring the Georgia history teacher had been challenged by a pastor at his church to go on a short-term mission trip. Not knowing what lay ahead, the teacher reluctantly agreed to go. When the team arrived in Panama, he was introduced to Itzel and assigned to work alongside her in her village to engage in house-to-house evangelism. At the end of their week together they were blessed to count

over 30 of Itzel's neighbors who had repented and put their
faith in Jesus, all meeting together in the center of the village under a tin roof to worship the Risen Lord.

Itzel's prayer had been answered. A church had been
planted within walking distance from her home. As you
can imagine, she was overcome with joy and subsequently
hosted a celebration outside her small cinderblock home
where she invited the new believers to say good-bye to the
high school teacher who had spent a week in their midst
sharing the gospel. It was there under the tree in Itzel's
front yard that they met and shared a meal together. As
the teacher ate his meal, his hands got a little messy so he
requested a napkin from his hostess. Itzel asked him to
wait just a moment. A few minutes passed and the teacher
repeated his request, moments after which he turned to see
Itzel's young daughter riding down that dusty dirt road on
her bicycle . . . with a single napkin in her hand. Itzel did
not have any napkins so she had sent her daughter down
to a small store to buy one. She thought it was the least
she could do to show gratitude to this young man that had
traveled from America to help her dream come true. As
the teacher sat there on that day something happened in
his life. Something dramatic. He was not sure exactly
what God was doing, but he knew life could never be the
same again in the light of the week's experiences.

Later that night he was at another celebration service
back in the city where Itzel had once traveled to attend
church services. A local pastor called for all the missionaries to come to the front of the auditorium so the church
could pray over them. The teacher sat in his seat still pon-

dering the eventful week. He sat there until someone behind him tapped him on the shoulder and said, "You go." Confused, the American replied, "I'm not a missionary. I'm a school teacher." The stranger spoke back to him with a smile on his face, "No. You are a missionary." It was in that moment the teacher realized he was a missionary. He had just invested a week of his life living out the Great Commission to make disciples and the Great Commandment to love God and love others. He thought, "Maybe I am a missionary."

He got on the plane the next day to go home to his beautiful fiancée, wondering what she would think about what God was doing in his heart. When she met him at the airport, she greeted him with a statement followed by a dangerous question. "There's something different about you. Are we going to be doing this the rest of our lives?" The young man replied shyly, "I think so." To his joy, his bride-to-be smiled at him and said, "Good. I told you I'd follow you anywhere, and I meant it."

Little did they know that just a year after their wedding they would be moving away to seminary so that he could pursue a degree in International Church Planting. Nor were they aware that his studies would take them to live in an Asian village among an unreached people that were 100% Shia' Muslim to engage them with the gospel. They had no idea they would arrive in that land with a nine-month-old son, and while there, give birth to a daughter. They could have never known that prior to the end of that first term her mother would be diagnosed with terminal cancer, resulting in their return to the U.S. to care for her. And who would have known that their growing passion for seeing God's glory among the nations would again be stoked when the teacher cum missionary would be asked to join the staff of the very ministry that took him on that first short-term mission journey years earlier?

You might have figured out by now that this is no second-hand story. This is a description of my own journey over the last dozen years. So much has happened in that relatively short span of time. Had my amazing wife and I known all God had planned for us, we probably would have balked at that initial act of obedience more than a decade ago. But in spite of all the challenges we have faced, we have known the pure joy of seeing countless men and women come to faith in Jesus and local churches established in nearly a half dozen countries spanning the globe.

God seldom gives the fullness of His plan all at once. We couldn't handle it. But He does shine a little light on the path in front of us revealing the next step of obedience. And then He waits for us to act upon the truth He has revealed. Such is the walk of faith. Life is an adventure when we seize God's Divine opportunities.

For the past five years I have had the joy of leading many people toward taking the initial step of faith into involvement in God's global plan of redemption at what has now become known as e3 Partners Ministries. e3 Partners exists to equip God's people to evangelize the lost and establish new indigenous churches. One of the primary components of the ministry's approach to fulfilling this mission statement is to use short-term mission teams as a catalytic force serving national church planting strategies. This is the model I was introduced to back in 1996 when I partnered with Itzel to help establish a church in her village.

I know what you're probably thinking. "Can a short-term mission team really establish a church in a week or two?" My response is, "No. But God can!" And He has literally thousands of times throughout the 20-year history of this ministry.

I'm often asked, "So what ever happened to Itzel and that church in Panama?" Joyfully I can write that I continue to correspond with Itzel and even had the privilege of her attendance at one of my church planting conferences a few years ago. The church? Itzel tells me that like any local church, there are challenges. However, the church continues to meet and has even reproduced by helping to start another church in a neighboring village.

Background

Several years ago I started working on a Doctor of Missiology degree at Western Seminary in Portland, Oregon. Many of the principles and ideas in this book come directly from my dissertation research where I used e3 Partners' model for establishing churches as a case study to determine if it is a viable and strategic use of the growing phenomenon of short-term missions. Rather than present those findings here in a technical and academic format, I have chosen to make the outcomes available in the context of a metaphor for ease of understanding. "Striking the Match" is intended for a much broader audience than my dissertation, including anyone involved in, affected by, or considering short-term missions and the role it should play in God's global plan of redemption. The research that served as the basis for my dissertation and this book was focused on how short-term mission teams at e3 Partners affect and are perceived by the nationals we work alongside.

Much has been written about the effects of short-term missions on those going. I do not feel compelled to speak to those issues primarily, but rather, I want to give a voice to my heroes in the majority world who are an inspiration to me as they live out the Great Commission. They are pastors, church planters and courageous lay leaders like Itzel. Regardless of your experience with short-term missions, what truly matters is that God's Kingdom be advanced through the establishment of healthy, reproducing indigenous churches.

Layout

It seems imperative that we as the people of God seek His face about how to properly use the resources He has given us, making sure what we are doing is in line with the Lord's commands. For this reason the first part of the book is dedicated to presenting the biblical, historical, and theological foundations of short-term missions. I begin with these subjects because I want to avoid my own cultural leanings toward pragmatism (ends justifying the means). By going first to the Scripture, and then on to Church history we can see how God has worked in the past. This provides a trustworthy framework for how He may choose to work in our midst today.

The second part of this book is dedicated to explaining how e3 Partners has learned to maximize the strategic impact of short-term mission teams by using them as catalysts in starting spiritual wildfires through partnering to ignite church planting movements. There are chapters on how to make the conditions right for a fire through indigenous leadership development, how to strike the match of the short-term mission team in such a way that it is not a wasted resource, and how to add fuel to the fire through interdependent partnerships long after the short-term team has completed its task. A brief overview of the research I conducted in 2005-2006 is provided along with some of the findings based upon the indigenous national hosts' perspectives.

The third part of this book is dedicated to providing the historical development of the ministry of e3 Partners and some of the empirical evidence that fires are actually being started through the strategic use of short-term mission teams. I set forth the premise that for STM to be strategic, it must be tied into a long-term strategy with its primary purpose being to help its national hosts reach their own people and beyond through reproductive church planting. There are many long-term mission organizations that focus on church planting; and there are many churches and organizations that mobilize laity to be involved in cross-cultural ministry. e3 Partners has sought to combine the catalytic manpower of STM with the focus of church planting in order to result in a strategic approach to cross-cultural missions. e3 Partners cannot take credit for much except that we recognized that the combination of STM and church planting is a match made in heaven.

Purpose and Audience

There are a plethora of valuable, Christ-exalting activities out there that constitute the estimated four million short-termers going out from North America annually. In this book you will read about one model that has proven to be quantitatively and qualitatively strategic from the perspective of the indigenous national hosts e3 Partners works to support and encourage. It is my prayer that by reading the story of how God has developed and used this ministry, you will be both challenged and encouraged to think strategically for the glory of God. If you are a pastor, you will find ideas here that will help you lead the army of ordinary people in your church to a Kingdom impact among the nations by engaging in something strategic and lasting. If you are a long-term missionary or a sending agency, you will find ideas that sharpen your understanding as to the best way to utilize the growing swell of volunteers God is sending your way as a catalytic component of your long-term church planting strategy. And if you are simply an ordinary follower of Jesus who wants to be used of God in a strategic way, this book will help you take the first steps toward Christ-exalting and Kingdom-focused obedience.

Part 1:
Remembering the Fires of the Past

The Biblical, Theological and Historical Development of Short-term Missions

Rome 64 AD. London 1666. Chicago 1871. San Francisco 1906. What do these locations and dates all have in common? Each of them was marked by fire. When historians look back at these cities and that particular year great fires stand out as the most significant event recorded. Great fires such as these have impacted tens of thousands of lives throughout human history. And great fires rage today as well. But all great fires begin with a simple spark.

What we know and understand about today's fires was learned by studying the fires of the past. And when it comes to spiritual wildfires, we should likewise look to the past and learn from our forebears. Physical fires destroy. Spiritual fires bring life. In the pages that follow I will introduce how God has worked in history to turn tiny sparks into great spiritual wildfires that have impacted millions including those of us reading this book.

Chapter 1

Where there's Smoke, there's Fire!

"I have come to bring fire on the earth, and how I wish it were already kindled!" **Luke 12:49**

We Need Fire

If you want to get people's attention all you have to do is scream "Fire!" The very word can illicit a range of emotions, depending upon the context within which it is spoken. Fire can be both destructive and helpful. Set loose in a building it brings a panic. Contained within a fireplace it sets a mood of relaxation. Why is that? Maybe it is because we as humans fear that which we can not control. Over the course of human history mankind has learned how to harness this force and use it for positive purposes. With regards to the harvest cycle, you often see farmers using fire to burn off the old growth, resulting in new life through enriching the soil. There are even some seeds that will not germinate without first being subjected to the heat of fire. The bottom line is that we need fire.

Fire in the Bible

Think about the Scripture. Fire is often used in the Bible to represent the presence of God. The firepot passing between the covenant sacrifice in Abram's journey (Genesis 15:17). For Moses there was both the burning bush (Exodus 3:2) and the pillar of fire by night (Exodus 13:21). Elijah saw fire come down from heaven and consume the sacrifice on Mt. Carmel (1 Kings 18:38), and he was also carried up to God in a chariot of fire (2 Kings 2:11). In Acts the Holy Spirit came upon the Apostles like tongues of fire (Acts 2:3). And eight times the Bible says that our God is a "consuming fire."

Some of the biblical references to fire are cast in a favorable light and others convey the holiness and the wrath of God. It should be noted however that God created fire and uses it for His own purposes. Like all of God's creation, it is only when we try to use something against God's purpose that it becomes corrupted. Take for example the unauthorized fire that Nadab and Abihu offered in Leviticus 10:1. The Scripture is very clear that their offering was "contrary to his (the Lord's) command." Interestingly enough, the two were consumed by the fire of God as a result of their misuse of the resource that had been given them.

We Need That Which We Fear

We fear fire, but we need it. So too, we should fear (have a healthy respect for) God. We desperately need Him. We need Him to personally ignite the fire of His presence in our lives. When that occurs we call it "revival." Revival is wonderful . . . when it is followed by radical obedience to the One who brings it. We desperately need to see God move beyond our own personal lives, and even beyond our existing churches. We need to see God spread a passion for His glory like a wildfire throughout this world. And in many places around the world He is doing just that by using radically obedient disciples. God is out starting wildfires.

Wildfires Around the World

What I'm referring to as a wildfire has become one of the newest focal points in current missions strategy and has been labeled by some as church planting movements (often referred to simply as "CPMs"). This phenomenon is by no means new in the sense that God never worked this way before. Rather the concept of CPMs has given modern day missions strategists a new way to describe how God is working to bring about the completion of the Great Commission. The descriptive term CPM was made popular back in the 1990s when David Garrison produced a small booklet on the subject that forced his own mission agency and many others to rethink their strategies. In that initial work, Garrison defined a CPM as "a rapid multiplication of indigenous churches planting churches that sweeps through a people group or population segment".[1]

The recognition of CPMs serves to illustrate a definitive evolution of mission strategy over the last century and has shifted our definition of success from winning converts one at a time through a ministry of addition, to seeing whole segments of people groups follow Jesus in a ministry of exponential multiplication. Many argue that this paradigm shift is actually a return to an apostolic understanding of what it means to obey the Great Commission. I think that we are just beginning to see what God is up to around the world. In some places fires are blazing.

The First Evidence of Fire

Much harsh criticism has been dealt toward short-term missions (STM) recently, and some of it justified. Field missionaries have grown frustrated with these "tour groups" coming in and snapping a few photos, doing a little work, and reinforcing the stereotype of the "ugly American". The question comes forth, "Is there such thing as strategic short-term missions?" Most missiologists would argue that if such a thing exists, it is indeed rare. Could it be that both critics and proponents alike have overestimated their own predictions regarding the phenomenon of STM? Who should be evaluating STM?

Missiologists? Mission Agencies? Or nationals who host STM teams?

We have all heard the old idiom "Where there's smoke there's fire." But do we believe it? In the original research that led to this publication, I argued that the national hosts are best equipped to tell us how to start fires in their own countries.[2] And if the nationals believe that they can use STM teams to start fires, who is going to argue with them? For this reason my research was based upon how the nationals themselves were impacted by the e3 Partners' model for church planting. Bits and pieces of that research are scattered throughout this book like smoke signals, but if you want to see the fires, you may just have to join e3 Partners on one of its journeys.[3]

Striking the Match

Chapter 2
I Am With You For A Short Time Only

Jesus said, "I am with you for only a short time, and then I go to the one who sent me." John 7:33

The Shaping Force of Western Rationalism

Culture touches everything. It is shaped by us and is at the same time shaping us. Our culture in the West has been molded by rationalism, the idea that truth is ascertained through reason and factual analysis rather than through faith or religious dogma. Neither those of us raised in North America nor North Americans living in the majority world escape the tentacles of our birth culture.[4] Even those in the Church have been influenced by

Western rationalism to the point that our theology and our lifestyles are sometimes affected. Theologically, many people have come to believe that God did miracles in the past, but are not so sure that the miraculous occurs in the "Modern" world. Have we forgotten that God chose ordinary men and women throughout history through which He would accomplish the miraculous for His glory? A.W. Tozer once said, "Anything that God has ever done at any other time, He can do now. Anything that God has ever done anywhere else, He can do here. And anything God has ever done for anyone else, He can do for me." Nice quote, but do you believe it? I do.[5]

Some Evangelical theologians and missionaries have been more impacted by this rationalistic worldview than they would like to admit. Ralph Winter articulated one of the more common arguments against short-term missions in saying that there is a great disparity between what can be accomplished in such a limited amount of time by "amateurs" and the amount of money that such trips require.[6] Skepticism is good when it is rooted in the Scripture. While Winter and a few others may see the re-amateurization of missions as an undesirable trend, I believe that it is in fact a return to biblical roots where the Spirit-filled laity was largely responsible for the rapid expansion of the Church. After all, the word *amateur* (Latin) actually translates "someone who acts out of love." One need not look far to learn that God often worked through imperfect biblical figures to accomplish a great deal in sometimes short and always purposeful visits. Think about Peter who saw God do the miraculous in a day. Peter was one of those unlearned men whose credentials amounted to time with Jesus. When Peter was filled with the Holy Spirit on the Day of Pentecost thousands were saved (Acts 2:41). Our Omnipotent God is not bound by time constraints or our limited abilities. The extra-ordinary God of the Bible still chooses to use ordinary men and women to accomplish His purposes in today's rationalistic world. Sometimes we just have a difficult time recognizing Him because our view has been blurred by Western rationalism. The bottom line is that if a particular missions strategy finds its basis in the Bible, then it should be utilized.

Ordinary and Extra-ordinary in the Old Testament

Our God is indeed a missionary God and the Bible is the Holy Spirit's documentation of the redemptive plan (*missio dei*) of God. The need for God's mission emerges early in the Genesis account after Adam and Eve's rebellion in the Garden (Genesis 3). No sooner had man fallen than God was already acting to restore according to the proto-evangelium (first mention of the gospel) found in Genesis 3:15. It was not until Genesis 12 and the Abrahamic Covenant, however, that God further explained how He would fulfill His mission to restore humanity. That restoration was not just a matter of proclamation, but rather a process culminating in the very incarnation of the Son of God. Filbeck avows, "God said it all in calling Abraham so that all clans and nations might be blessed because of him. After that, it was mainly a matter of working out the details . . . ."[7]

The Redemptive plan of God is truly extra-ordinary. However, the people He chose to use to move that plan along make for a long list people who were, at best, ordinary. All along the way those who were God's ordinary people engaged in "missions" as a part of God's larger story of Redemption. The book *Maximum Impact Short-Term Missions* lists several of these assignments that involved a relatively short duration of time, citing them as evidence of STM in the Old Testament. Among them are the two angels' deliverance mission in Sodom and Gomorrah (Genesis 18-19), Moses' confrontation of Pharoah and subsequent liberation of God's People (Exodus 3-12), the Hebrew spies going into Canaan on a fact-finding mission, Elijah and the Widow of Zarephath (1 Kings 17), Nehemiah's short-term construction trip (Nehemiah 2-10), and many others.[8] All of these may not correspond with what we now call modern STM. The authors may have overstated their case in their zeal to make a point. I do, however, believe they prove that God can, when He so desires, accomplish a great deal toward His purposes in a short time with what could be considered ordinary people.

One of the premiere missionary texts within the OT is the story of Jonah. In the biblical account, the missionary Jonah was sent cross-culturally to preach repentance to the citizens of Nineveh and saw tremendous results in a very short period of time. The people and the king seem to have heard the message and repented in a single day (Jonah 3:4-5). The emphasis here is not on what Jonah did in a day, but rather what God did. Jonah preached reluctantly hoping the Ninevites would not repent. God, in His mercy led them to repentance in spite of Jonah rather than because of him. In missions circles we are often too quick to take the credit for what God accomplished, whether in a lifetime of dedicated service or on a one week STM journey. All of us ordinary people need to be careful to give our extra-ordinary God the credit due Him for anything eternal that flows from our lives. And we also must be careful to ascribe to God the Omnipotence that is His. After all, God chose to create all we see in the physical realm in just six days. If He could create the Universe in six days *ex nihilo* (out of nothing), only a mind influenced by Western rationalism would doubt that He could, or would choose to do something significant and of eternal value through ordinary people He calls to be His children. The point here is that it is God's mission and He has chosen to use different means to accomplish it, as well as different lengths of time.

A Long-term Missionary that Used Short-term Missions as Strategy

No other man has ever lived who listened to, was led by, and obeyed the voice of God the Father more than the God-man, Jesus Christ. On the one hand, Jesus epitomizes the long-term incarnational approach to missions by coming to earth in the form of man and in the context of human culture, planting his life among the humanity he desired to reach. On the other hand, within the context of eternity – or even human history for that matter – Jesus limited his stay on earth to 33 years, only in the last three of which he served openly in the public realm. Three years of public ministry is very short-term considering all he came to accomplish! He was candid with His disciples when he said, "I am with you for only a short time, and then I go to the one who sent me" (John 7:33). His thirty-three-year incarnation was central to his age-old plan for global redemption. I would by no means say that STM should always be central to LTM strategy as if it were indispensable. But I think the Incarnation does communicate, at least to some degree, that Jesus is a LTM that used STM in His own strategy.

Bryan Slater notes that Jesus not only took the initiative to call his disciples and send them out (Matthew 10), but he also had previously and adequately modeled all they would need to do as they went (Mark 1:39 and Luke 8:1-3).[9] Slater goes on to note that Jesus initiated the disciples' STM, gave them specific training, prepared the way for their mission, and provided thorough debriefing following the mission.[10] Thus Jesus had a larger, comprehensive strategy with the disciples built upon many shorter term endeavors.

Following the sending of the Twelve, Jesus sent out a group known as the Seventy-two in a similar manner (Luke 10:1). Randall Friesen seems to believe that one of Jesus' primary purposes in sending the disciples was as a means of training and enrichment. "(This) short-term mission was connected to Jesus' broader mission and was only possible because He had called, trained and sent these disciples."[11] Thus, in IIis relatively short life on earth Jesus fully accomplished the will and mission the Father had planned for Him (John 17:4). However, the *missio dei* gave birth to "missions" through the commissioning and training of the disciples. Missions is the continuation of Jesus' strategy in the Father's global plan of redemption. "All of history is moving toward one great goal, the white-hot worship of God and His Son among all the peoples of the earth. Missions is not that goal. It is the means."[12]

The Role of Short-term Missions in the Strategy of Paul

Some refer to the Apostle Paul as the greatest missionary the church has ever known. Much of what we understand about missions from the Scripture we derive from the ministry of Paul. It is widely accepted that he seldom stayed longer than a few months or even weeks in a single location, with a few notable exceptions in Ephesus (2.5 years) and Corinth (1.5 years).[13] This being the case, many that work in STM have heralded Paul as their champion and seem to believe that if the strategy were good enough for Paul, it should be good enough for missionaries today. One must be careful of making too close of a comparison, however, because although Paul never planted himself for life in one location (the "modern" missions standard), he made a lifetime commitment to missions at the outset of his ministry and continued sacrificially in that calling until his death. A. Wayne Meece reasons that Paul's short-terms were not of his own devising but were necessitated by circumstance. He goes on to say:

> *It was not Paul's practice to spend a week or two in a place, baptize a few people, organize a church, appoint elders and then leave them on their own. Those who do so and use Paul as their example misunderstand Paul and his methods altogether.*[14]

Meece's argument ends, however, with the idea that STM should not replace LTM, but rather be utilized to supplement the overall missionary cause. So it seems that Paul, like Jesus, was a long-term missionary that at the very least incorporated STM thinking into his strategy.

STM today is often treated as an opportunity for people to test-drive a calling in missions; to "try it on for size." That is not even close to Paul's STM strategy. Instead, Paul took small teams along with him, establishing churches and appointing national leaders from one location to the next. He continued in a mentoring or coaching role through return visits, sending others in his stead or writing letters addressing specific needs of congregations where he had influence. Missiologist Roland

Allen, in his classic *Missionary Methods: St. Paul's or Ours?* notes that much good can be accomplished in a short amount of time when missionaries empower the nationals to reach their own people.[15] Again, the question is not that of duration of stay, but rather of purpose and strategy. Miles believes, however, that Allen's statements need not be taken as an endorsement of the modern phenomenon of STM because "he was saying that the long-term missionary could achieve a lot (in a short time) and move on to other places . . . ."[16] In essence, Paul was a long-term missionary using STM as his primary strategy. Slater states, "Like Paul, short-term missionaries today must see each project as one stop in a longer journey."[17] Those who truly desire their STM to be strategic must begin to think like the Apostle Paul.

In total, the Apostle Paul's missionary journeys spanned less than 15 years after which he declared, "So from Jerusalem all the way around to Illyricum, I have fully proclaimed the gospel of Christ" (Romans 15:19), going on to set his sights on Spain.[18] Early in the modern STM movement, Donald Kitchen asserted:

> *Paul . . . was constantly changing his field of ministry . . . (staying) time periods that today would be considered as only a brief visit to the mission field . . . (but) was used of God to plant churches in four different provinces of the Empire, spanning two continents in less than ten years.*[19]

Meece seems to believe that the narratives of Paul's missionary journeys in the Book of Acts are illusive when it comes to the amount of time spent in each location. He reiterates that Paul revisited most locations time and again and that the great missionary seldom left a city of his own accord but was usually forced to leave because of persecution.[20] Regardless of Meece's call for reexamination of Paul's length of term, the fact remains that Paul's ministry had a great deal in common with those engaged in STM today as a part of a longer-term field-based strategy. We have no evidence that Paul attempted to study or communicate in the local indigenous languages. We have no evidence that he ever intended to go to one particular place and plant his life there among one group of people. This is not to say that such LTM strategies are wrong. Rather, this is just a notation that such practices were not foundational to the church planting strategy of the Apostle Paul. The fact is, in today's world LTM and STM are becoming more integrated and the result is that the Kingdom of God is advancing in ways the world has not seen since the First Century.

Other New Testament Examples

The Book of Acts was written as a narrative by Luke in order to document the origins of the Church of Jesus Christ. Found within the Book of Acts are a myriad of stories detailing the early Church's approach to mission, or rather the Holy Spirit's approach to mission in using the early Church. A key that arises from the Book of Acts is that in spite of "signs and wonders" and the grand personalities, the Holy Spirit intended that the entirety of the community of Christ-followers be engaged in the mission of God. Church historian Michael Green stresses, "these disciples of Jesus believed in every member ministry."[21] Green argues that the Book of Acts is a documentation of how God used informal, unqualified, and ordinary people to spread the Gospel both near and far.[22] Some things never change.

The story of Philip and the Ethiopian eunuch found in Acts 8:26-40 would certainly fit the model of short-term mission – less than one day to be exact – conducted by one of the "unlearned men" that followed Jesus! Philip was commissioned by an angel and Spirit-led in his encounter with the devout seeker. Slater touches on the fact that, "(Philip) was uniquely prepared for the mission: He had served time as a deacon (Acts 6:3-7), so he had been tested and was a mature disciple of Christ. He had the gift of an evangelist (Acts 21:8), so this calling fit him perfectly."[23] Interestingly, the Book of Acts documents several more stops for Philip prior to his arrival and subsequent ministry in Caesarea which may have lasted over 20 years.[24] This type of "hit and run" encounter may not be normative, but we do get the impression that many of the participants in the Book of Acts were constantly on the move. Once again, historian Michael Green contends that these short stays showed a degree of trust toward the new Christians that were won, and even more so, a trust in the God who brought them to the truth.[25]

With God All Things Are Possible

Looking at the Scripture, the amount of time invested on the part of the servant of God may be of less importance than most missiologists presume. What stands out is that God can do anything He chooses in either a short or long period of time, sometimes through His servants and at other times in spite of them! The Bible is replete with examples where God did use short-term assignments, sometimes with untrained and non-professional ministers, to accomplish His redemptive plan. Thus it is aptly stated in *Maximum Impact Short-term Missions*, "If short-term mission does have a solid Biblical basis, then cognitive logic fabricated for or against the use of short-term mission is rendered mute."[26] A truly biblical missions strategy doesn't force us to choose between STM and LTM as if they are mutually exclusive. Rather, a biblical strategy includes both STM and LTM in a symbiotic relationship. Jesus says, "With man this is impossible, but not with God; all things are possible with God" (Mark 10:27).

Chapter 3
Remember Way Back When?

"Missionary work, though it may occupy a missionary's life-time, is essentially temporary in nature." **Harold Cook**

What Goes Around Comes Around

In the last chapter we saw that our extra-ordinary God can and does work through ordinary people like you and me to accomplish His mission. The biblical basis of God's using these ordinary individuals often for rela-tively short terms as part of His long-term strategy was established. In this chapter we will build upon that biblical basis and look at the historical roots of this phe-nomenon today referred to as STM.

Most of the literature in the field of STM traces the current trend back to the 1960s with the founding of Operation Mobilization (OM) and Youth With a Mission (YWAM).[27] While those two organizations deviated somewhat from the traditional residential missionary role, a closer look at church history will show that itinerate missions have been common since apostolic times.

John Mark Terry has identified several factors that affected the Church's expansion following the close of the biblical canon.[28] Chief among those factors was the excellent road system within the Roman Empire. Along with the ease of travel was the safety that accompanied the Pax Romana and the widespread use of the Greek language. Two final factors mentioned by Terry are the spread of Greek philosophy, which valued truth and devalued superstition, and the diaspora of Jews and synagogues throughout the Empire that made the witness of the Old Testament and practice of monotheism acceptable. Interestingly, parallels to these very conditions seem to be behind the modern spread of the Church as well as the phenomenon of STM. Could it be that God is once again aligning various cultural conditions for a massive thrust forward in the expansion of the Church?

Cultural Parallels with the Past

The recent advent of safe, frequent, and affordable air travel to virtually any place on the planet, along with the rise of democracy, and the spread of English as a global language, seem to be factors in the global growth of the Church in our own times. *Maximum Impact* adds to the list of contemporary causes the advent of the Peace Corps in the 1960s by which the U.S. government challenged young people to get involved globally, as well as the creation of the Internet connecting us with people in a virtual global community making distant lands (and field missionaries for that matter) accessible.[29] I would add to these commonalities the expanse of cultural influence the Roman Empire had in the first three centuries of Christianity and the advent of the USA as a force in world politics and social influence in the 20th century. The difference between the two scenarios would be that Rome had its influence and then used it to some degree to make Christianity a world religion, whereas the USA had Christianity as a cultural norm prior to gaining global political super-power status. Both, at least for a period, made it acceptable within their sphere of cultural influence to become "Christian."

Even with these large-scale influences, the Gospel travels in the context of personal interaction from one person to another. Terry notes that several early church historians such as Eusebius, Origen, and Clement testified to the influence of itinerant missionaries traveling from city to city and throughout even remote areas making converts and starting churches.[30] It seems several early Bishops were even itinerants at

times.[31] However most of the growth in those early
years can be attributed to what Terry calls "lay missionaries" who were "Christian traders evangeliz(ing)
as they traveled through the empire."[32] The spread of
the Church westward beyond the daily influence of the
Roman Empire depended far more upon lay leadership
and itinerant workers than upon those who held official
positions within the Church.

Men in Skirts Make Great Church Planters

George G. Hunter III argues that the growth of the
Celtic church was "more of a movement than an institu-
tion . . . featuring laity in ministry more than clergy."[33]
Because the Celts were a nomadic people the church
had to be flexible and mobile. And wherever Celtic
Christians traveled they took the Gospel along with
them, usually staying only a short time before moving
along. Within a few generations they had permeated
all of Ireland with the Gospel and began to work cross-
culturally in what is now England, and among other
tribes as well. Hunter claims that "by the eleventh century their 'culturally relevant' movement had adapted
Christianity to the language and culture of many different Celtic and Germanic peoples . . . ."[34] Keep in mind
that these missionaries were neither trained professionals, nor did they typically plant themselves in any one
location for a length of time. They were traders and
nomads sharing the transforming message of the
Gospel in obedience to the Great Commission. They

were quite successful amateurs who seem to have used a hybrid approach to mission incorporating both STM and LTM. If we are going to advance the Kingdom of God today we would do well to learn from these historical forebears. It was not the skirts that made the Celts successful Kingdom agents, it was their flexibility and missional approach to life.

Modernity Redefined Missions

So how does our modern missions strategy fare in light of the Book of Acts? In a rather insightful comment John Miles notes, "The modern LTM strategy has more in common with the 'evangelization by migration' experience of the early Christians who were persecuted . . . " rather than being based upon the documented intentional methodology of the apostles that moved about spreading the Gospel.[35] William Carey is often called the "Father of Modern Missions." Born in England in the late 18th century, Carey was quite the pioneer of a relatively "new" methodology, intentional long-term residential missions. Carey's ministry in India has had a tremendous impact on the modern view of missions. Obviously very astute, Carey managed in his 40-year career to translate the complete Bible into six languages, the New Testament into nearly 30 languages yet saw "only a few thousand" Indian converts.[36] Baar notes that Carey "modeled the life of a missionary to the Christian world . . . He lived and worked among the Indian people."[37] I am personally indebted to Carey because the tens of thousands of New Testaments I have distributed on STM journeys in South Asia were a result of his commitment to plant his life there. Could it be that a not-so-subtle paradigm shift in missionary methods took place in the wake of this "modern" missionary hero?[38] A shift from missions as a fluid and nomadic way of life to missions as a more stationary lifestyle? Carey and the multitudes that have followed his lead over the last two hundred years have sacrificially laid a broad foundation upon which the current STM movement has been built. Apart from the advances that long-term missionaries have made through their lifelong Spirit-led investments in foreign lands, most people who participate in STM today would not know where to go, whom to work with, or what to do. Rather than juxtaposing LTM and STM against one another, it seems God may have a both/and approach to missions, not the oft-argued either/or. We need to utilize all means possible – both LTM and STM – in the power of the Spirit to see God's global plan of redemption fulfilled.

In the generation following Carey, two student-initiated groups began with the purpose of raising up and sending out missionaries. First, the Student Foreign Missions Fellowship was founded at the Haystack Revival, and later associated primarily with Samuel Mills.[39] On its heels came the Student Volunteer Movement (SVM) that continued to expand and influence young people to commit their lives to missions into the turn of the 20th century. It was the SVM that coined the missiological watchword "The Evangelization of the World in this Generation."[40] By the time of the SVM, missions had become dominated by a paternalistic approach as missionaries were sometimes unintentional agents of colonialism. The SVM did not do away with the LTM approach by any means. It did, however, introduce a new sense of urgency into missions that no doubt caused missionaries to envision what it would be like to finish the task. Through the SVM more than 20,000 missionaries were sent into the world, many of which would remain for a lifetime.[41] But finishing the task was and still is an impossibility when it is contingent solely upon the sending and sustaining of long-term missionaries who have become trained professionals. The very thought that the task can and should be finished sooner rather than later beckons the involvement of the multitudes, something only possible through the symbiotic use of STM and LTM as a part of an over-arching strategy. I believe God was behind the wave of "amateurs" going out during the Student Volunteer Movement, and I believe God is behind the current wave in the STM movement as well.

A Paradigm Shift?

The last three decades have seen tremendous growth and change in missionary strategy, much of which can be attributed to the ease and availability of global travel. Prior to the 1970s international travel was very limited.[42] With the expansion of and increased competition between global commercial airlines, more and more people are venturing out and being exposed to other cultures. It is estimated by the U.S. Federal Aviation Administration that international air travel will nearly double in the first sixteen years of this millennium.[43] Fueling this trend is the emergence of an entire industry for tourists as people spend more of their leisure time abroad. This has resulted in greater accessibility to the mission fields of the world.

When evaluating the role of short-term missions (STM) flowing naturally from the increase in international travel, Wesley Paddock noted that in the Christian Standard STM participants rose from 10% of the overall missionary force to 40% between 1970 and 1992.[44] The number increased continually over the last decade. By the year 2000, John Kyle of the Evangelical Foreign Missions Association estimated the number of Western STMers to be nearly a half million.[45] Roger Peterson of STEM International (Short-term Evangelical Missions) posits that the number is likely more than twice that when all of the STM variations and sending entities are taken into consideration.[46] With so many STMers going out this trend is bound to make an impact. Whether that impact is positive or negative depends on whether we use this army of ordinary people as a strategic part of a long-term field-based strategy.

Paradigm Shifted

This paradigm shift toward increased utilization of STM demands further investigation to analyze its true impact for all parties. Two decades ago this growth was anticipated when one missologist wrote, "Christians need to see that a giant for the cause of Christ is striding among us. It's called the short-term missionary movement."[47] Friesen notes that this dramatic increase in STM participation coupled with the decline of long-term mission (LTM) involvement could be one of the most significant changes in modern missions.[48] It is by no means necessary for this "giant" to contribute to the demise of the residential role that has provided the missiological foundation over the last two centuries. We have seen in this chapter that the historical record reveals that STM and LTM can and should function together in Kingdom advancement. Following a chapter on the theological foundationd of STM, Parts Two and Three of this book attempt to show that by contributing to the church planting efforts of national leadership, STM can indeed be strategic.

Striking the Match

Chapter 4
Every Disciple a Church Planter

But you are a chosen people, a royal priesthood, a holy nation, a people belonging to God, that you may declare the praises of him who called you out of darkness into his wonderful light. **1 Peter 2:9**

It's God's Mission

The previous chapters established that the concept of STM is biblically based and to some degree grounded in historical precedent. STM is also a theologically sound approach to missions. It would be difficult to determine the theological grounding of missions without first defining "mission." Van Rheenan identifies mission simply as ". . . the work of God."[49] Our God is a missionary God.[50]

His mission began before the foundation of the world and part of that mission is the redemption and restoration of His fallen image-bearers. This broad theme is referred to as *missio dei*. Missions is essentially the role of God's restored people within the larger *missio dei*. We get the missions from the Latin *missio*, which carries the connotation of being sent (by God). Baar records that,

> *If mission is God's work in the world and missions are the plans of believers to carry out that mission, then a missionary is someone who is actively doing God's work; someone who is preaching the Gospel and making disciples, regardless of the specific methods that are used to do so.*[51]

It's Your Mission

In the past, missions has been relegated to the background in the local church primarily because pastors and church members did not understand how to get involved. I remember living in South Asia wishing my own sending church understood why I was there; however, they could not because they were unintentionally disconnected by virtue of cultural distance. I was serving in a valley where there were two believers – me and my wife! Of course, we had our seventeen-month-old son, Aidan, and our one-month-old daughter Tori Beth. The nearest believers were our best friends, the Powells, who were working with us to engage an unreached people group. We got to see them about twice a month when we met with them for worship. We did get the opportunity to

drive to the closest city (about 2.5 hours away) each
Monday to the closest telephone so we could send and
receive e-mail, quite the luxury. It took an average of
three hours just to complete that process. Each week I
tried to communicate all that God was doing in our little
valley tucked away at the ends of the earth. And each
week I responded to questions from people at my home
church in an effort to create understanding. It was then I
realized the only way people could possibly get a grasp on
what we were doing was to come for a visit. Those who
came learned that the missions mandate to the local
church involves more than just praying and giving. It
involves participation in the completion of the Great
Commission through making disciples of all nations.

God's mission is your mission! Jesus' last words to
His disciples as documented in Matthew's account of the
Great Commission are both powerful and empowering:

*All authority in heaven and on earth has been given to
me. Therefore go and make disciples of all nations,
baptizing them in the name of the Father and of the
Son and of the Holy Spirit, and teaching them to obey
everything I have commanded you. And surely I am
with you always, to the very end of the age.
(Matthew 28:18-20)*

These words are powerful in that the Great Commission
is based upon the authority of Christ. Jesus Christ has
entrusted the task of making disciples to His followers
and He has guaranteed our success with His own pres-

ence. When He beckoned His disciples to "teach them to observe all that I have commanded you," He was issuing the Great Commission to all of His followers. I take that to mean that every Christ-follower is to be engaged in the completion of the Great Commission, including making disciples cross-culturally. That is precisely where the power of STM comes into play. If everyone in the local church left their secular employment and moved to a cross-cultural mission field there would be no one to financially support the enterprise, and there would be no sending churches with whom to partner. There would be no one to engage the mission in their "Jerusalem and Judea." With STM, however, participation in the Great Commission is within the reach of any Christ-follower.

The Great Commission Is the Foundation of Missions

Over the last few centuries the focus of missions has broadened in scope to include activities such as education, healthcare, and social work. A cursory look at any sending agency website will show that one can engage in just about any type of activity under the banner of missions.[52] The biblical corpus however, leans toward the idea that missions itself should be defined by having an evangelistic or discipling orientation. Those other ministries should flow naturally from new believers being properly discipled in the context of a local church. This is not to say that contributions to education, healthcare, and social ministries are not valuable parts of living the Christ life.

They are crucial components of cultural transformation
and Kingdom expansion. But they should never replace
the primacy among missionaries of proclamation. The
world needs Christian doctors and nurses that proclaim
Christ while extending His healing hands. The world
needs Christian educators that proclaim Christ as the
embodiment of wisdom and the only hope of salvation.
The world needs Christian social workers that proclaim
Christ as the Bread of Life, the Living Water, and the
Giver of all good things. I am emphatically not devaluing
those exercising their gifts among the nations. I am simply saying that unless Christ is being proclaimed, those
activities are not distinctively missionary in nature
because missions hinges on proclamation.

Much of STM today would not be characterized as
missions according to my own conservative parameters.
Beyerhaus represents my position well in saying,
"Mission occurs when – and only when – it is directed
towards putting man's existence, through a conscious
decision of faith . . . the planting and growth of the church
as the body of Christ in the world remains the primary
goal of mission."[53]   I prefer to call STM that focuses on
construction or health or any other aspect divorced from
proclamation, a "work trip." There are legitimate needs
in those areas, but the vast majority of cursory internet
searches for short-term mission trips return a long list of
activities, very few of which involve calling people to
repentance and faith or establishing new churches.[54]

The Priesthood of Believers

The doctrine of the priesthood of believers is derived in part from 1 Peter 2:9, "But you (all) are a chosen race, a royal priesthood, a holy nation, a people for his own possession, that you may proclaim the excellencies of him who called you out of darkness into his marvelous light" (ESV). Unfortunately, the priesthood of believers has been neglected on both sides of many Western pulpits, and in some cases, our mission agencies. We "professionals" have neutered many of our churches by eliminating any real need for involvement. Church members have settled on being a passive group of observers that leave the work to the "experts." Peterson, Aeschliman and Sneed add that the problem has gone beyond the mission agency and has now entrenched itself in academia where it seems the Great Commission is now being interpreted as a job only for trained professionals.[55] Missiologist J. Herbert Kane warns mission agencies and academicians alike that the professionalism that has come to characterize missions over the last century will fade as the Great Commission becomes, once again, the common task of church members around the world, partly through participation in STM.[56] Peterson, Aeschliman and Sneed insist that "No worldwide strategy exists today to comply with this doctrine (of the priesthood of believers) – except the menacing, chancy tactic we call short-term mission."[57] In his own commentary on the doctrine, Filbeck concludes that as God's treasured possession, all of the people of

God are to both serve God and serve before God in behalf of others through participating in the ministry of reconciliation and redemption.[58] If we desire to see the Great Commission fulfilled, we must use all resources and all means at all costs. That includes the one mission strategy viable for every believer's total participation – STM.

The Mobilization Mandate

The power of STM is that it mobilizes whole churches to fully engage in Great Commission ministry. That is how I received the call to full-time missions ministry. An increasing number of field missionaries confess that were it not for a short-term journey, they may not have committed their lives to joining God's mission in a distant land. Thus, strategic STM may in fact be the best recruiting tool available to attract and identify potential full-time missionaries, or it may act as a filter to deter those who might otherwise have joined a mission only to come home soon after.[59] When local churches engage in cross-cultural ministry they are much more likely to become sending churches.

Pastor and author Bob Roberts, Jr. takes offense to what he describes as an unscriptural approach to missions, namely agencies and organizations trying to do missions by proxy on behalf of the local church. Roberts, who founded an organization called GlocalNet to bring the global mission back into the local church, believes that churches themselves are missionary by nature and that his job as a pastor is to help all believers to find their place in God's global mission.[60]

Roberts is not the only pastor attempting to bring the mission back into the local church by empowering its members. Best-selling author Rick Warren has thrown his weight behind the paradigm shift as well with his P.E.A.C.E. Plan, which aims to mobilize one billion people. The website set up to promote this gargantuan attempt says, "P.E.A.C.E. is not a church program for a few 'specialists' . . . (but) is a lay movement designed to mobilize average church members to do normal tasks that can change the world."[61] One might think that anything to get more people involved in God's redemptive mission would be welcomed. But as with any challenge to an existing methodology, those advocating such a grassroots and lay-driven approach to missions are not without their detractors. Ralph Winter states, "(Missions) has become any Christian volunteering to be sent anywhere in the world at any expense to do anything for any time period."[62] As already noted, I am all for delineating between missions and work trips. So I would agree with Winter that we need to be strategic with regard to where we are going and what we are doing once we are there. We must be careful, however, not to define missions by the amount of time invested. Time is not the foundation of strategy. Activity is. Church planting can be the goal of LTM and STM alike.

The bottom line is that as "believer priests" we are all commanded to go and make disciples of the nations.

Some will be more naturally adept; the Spiritual gifts of those who go often differ; but in the end it is God who is on mission. He doesn't call the qualified; He qualifies the called. I once heard Erwin McManus say that Jesus only has one call – "Come follow me."[63] In some respects we have created an artificial barrier between professional missionaries and the so-called laity as if Jesus had called some to stay and some to go. The only time Jesus told the disciples to stay was when they were to wait upon the indwelling of the Holy Spirit in Jerusalem. However, once they were filled and empowered, all of them were commanded to go. This principle remains true for followers of Christ today. If Jesus told us to go, why are the multitudes continuing to stay?

You? Plant a Church?

I once heard a dear Indian brother say, "Every believer a disciple. Every disciple a church planter. And every church a training center." He gets it! He bases his understanding for what is normative in the life of a believer upon solid theological underpinnings. STM is indeed a theologically sound approach to missions. While it is true that believers are gifted differently and called by God to play specific roles within the Body of Christ, this in no way negates the fact that we have been commissioned to make disciples of all nations. Friesen is correct in stating, "The methodology of 'short-term' must be connected to the long-term '*missio ecclesiato*' and must be seen within the even broader *'missio dei'*."[64]   Peterson et al aptly conclude:

> ***Missio Ecclesiato*** *must conform to* ***Missio Dei****. Any man-made plan of mission which sidesteps real, average believers who are already appointed as God's salt and light, overtly circumvents the design of God. Therefore it behooves us to ask the obvious question: are we structuring our Great Commission efforts to purposely include the foolish, the weak, the low, and the despised (i.e., the real people) in our churches? If not – then according to God's Word – we are refusing to conduct* ***Missio Dei*** *God's way.*[65]

Thus, the ultimate goal of all missionary enterprise, LTM or STM, should be the completion of the Great Commission. The most effective means to do this is arguably through planting churches that make disciples and multiply.[66] Greg Livingstone defines church planting as, "the whole process of evangelizing, discipling, training, and organizing a group of believers to a level of development permitting it to function as a viable church independent of the agents who brought it into being."[67] Through strategic STM, disciples are connected to the mission of the church and engaged in the mission of God. Even you can become a church planter!

Part 2
Fire Starting 101

e3 Partners' Model for Church Planting Using Strategic Short-term Mission Teams

Church planting movements are similar to wildfires in that both have a small beginning but given the right conditions, they rage and spread to affect everything around them. Spiritually speaking, the goal of any missionary regardless of length of term should be to start a "wildfire" that literally changes the cultural landscape of the target area. Most of the time, however, wildfires do not just happen. There must be a source or a catalytic event.

Sometimes wildfires are started through a lightning strike without the help of man at all. Church planting is definitely the work of God. God alone brings life to the spiritually dead by setting hearts ablaze for His glory. So at times throughout history God has moved in areas almost in spite of human efforts, rather than because of them. However, in His sovereign grace, the LORD often chooses to use His children as fire starters. In the pages that follow we will focus on how all Christ-followers can and should take part in God's mission to set the nations ablaze.

Striking the Match

Chapter 5
A Balancing Act

"with your blood you purchased men for God from every
tribe and language and people and nation".

Revelation 5:9

Working Toward a Balanced Strategy

Church was God's idea and it was a good one. People
from every tribe, every language, every people, and every
nation will make up the Body of Christ. There is tremendous diversity within the Body. There must also be
tremendous unity. While the Church may be made up of
individuals, missions strategy has no room for self-cen-
teredness on the part of any of its participants. That has
been one of the greatest problems in the current short-

term missions movement, and in the greater global missionary cause as a whole.

Peterson, Aeschlimann and Sneed introduce the Participant Trilogy in their book Maximum Impact Short-term Missions as an attempt to bring balance to the approach of STM (See Figure 1).[68] The authors point out that STM has become unbalanced, too often placing all the emphasis on either the goer-guest, or the sender, or the recipient-host.[69] The ideal strategy incorporating short-term mission teams would place value on all three of these roles and allow them to work together in reciprocity or better yet, interdependency. I would add that because the mission is ultimately God's, His Word should be at the center of any strategy. All parties must look to the Scripture first and foremost in development of a missions strategy.

Figure 1: STM Participant Trilogy

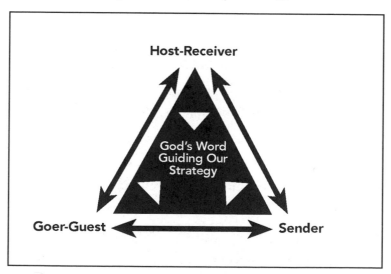

I believe there has been a "catch 22" when it comes to who benefits from STM. If the STM is focused too much on benefits for the goer-guest participation can become hedonistic in nature. Hedonism refers to indulgence in self-pleasure or fulfillment as a primary motive. "Missiological hedonism" is a term I coined to describe situations where a person's primary motive for engaging in missions is what they might get out of it. The vast majority of the literature available on STM has this goer-guest orientation. J. Herbert Kane wrote early in the emergence of the current STM movement noting that it is inherently goer-centered. He lists four advantages for the goer-guest :[70]

1. It enables him to better understand the aims and goals of the missionary.
2. It provides an enriching exposure to a different culture.
3. It acquaints him with the enormous difficulties faced by a Christian church – often an isolated, sometimes persecuted, minority – in a non-Christian environment.
4. It helps him to ascertain the will of God for his life.

Most of the literature written by STM advocates deals with either team orientation, utilizing the trip as a tool for spiritual growth of the participants, or prolonging the personal impact of the trip. These goals are not wrong, they are just not to be central in our planning and evaluation of missions.

STM Orientation-Outcome Matrix

Orientation	Strengths	Weaknesses	Outcomes
Goer-guest	Spiritual growth	Culturally insensitive	Hedonistic
Recipient-host	Culturally appropriate Church growth	Dependency issues	Paternalistic
Sender	Mobilization public relations	Self-preservation Means becomes the end	Commercialistic
Interdependence	Reciprocity on all levels	-----	Kingdom growth via Strategic STM

In observing another potential orientation of STM, if focused too much on the recipient-hosts mission can easily become a paternalistic endeavor. This is exemplified in the myriad of mission projects that do good on the surface but end up creating unhealthy dependency thereby removing dignity from the very people the project was meant to serve. Once dependency is created there is rarely an easy way out for either party. The result is almost always an attitude of resentment toward the benefactor and eventually bad feelings emerge on all sides.

Both of the aforementioned orientations have been addressed to some degree throughout the years, but there is a relatively new orientation; focusing too much on benefiting the sending agency/church. In these cases mission can become shamelessly commercial. Although more subtle, this orientation is becoming more of an issue as increasing competition emerges between sending entities. Those of us in leadership must guard our hearts to make sure we do not allow the mission to be supplanted by marketing.

The only solution to these focal tensions is to work toward what I call missiological interdependence, whereby all of the members of the Participant Trilogy work for the benefit of the others and all are blessed as a result through reciprocity. If STM is to ever reach its potential for being strategic an interdependent focus will need to come to the forefront of the movement. This means senders will need to orient teams on all three levels: being culturally appropriate with recipient-hosts, growing spiritually on a personal level, and continuing in partnership with the sending entity to maximize the impact. For goer-guests this means placing the needs of the recipients and the vision of the sending entity above their own. For sending entities this means making the long-term benefits of both STM participants and national partners the foundation of strategy. And for recipient-hosts this means working with senders to develop meaningful strategies for using STM teams. These goals are lofty, but achievable. Jesus commanded us to think this way in the Great Commandment in Luke 10:27; "Love the Lord your God with all your heart and with all your soul and with all your strength and with all your mind and, love your neighbor as yourself." That verse should sum up any mission strategy. God is central. Others before ourselves.

The Church will continue to expand and churches will continue to multiply because Jesus has purchased for God through His atoning sacrifice men and women from every tongue, tribe, and nation. The Great Commission is going to be fulfilled. The question is will we be actively engaged in its fulfillment for the glory of Christ? If so, we must learn to perform a balancing act in the development of our mission strategy, one that uses the Great Commandment as the key to the Great Commission!

Chapter 6
Playing with Fire?

If their purpose or activity is of human origin, it will fail.
But if it is from God, you will not be able to stop these
men; you will only find yourselves fighting against God.

Acts 5:38b-39

The Purpose of a Match

Parents ages ago came up with a warning that addresses
the inexplicable draw of their children toward starting
fires. "Don't play with matches!" Why? A person that has
interest in matches without much knowledge about fires
can really cause a lot of problems. Import that age-old
warning from mom into the metaphor that serves as the
framework for this book. I have argued that God often

uses ordinary people to accomplish extra-ordinary things. Not everyone, however, is equal in knowledge and ability in starting the wildfires of a CPM. The admonition of not playing with matches applies to many who are involved short-term work without first being educated on the nature of fire. Too many people are striking matches and tossing them to the ground without any idea of how to truly start a fire. Many have forgotten that the purpose of a match is to start something that outlasts the initial burst of flame. Some have taken a precious resource and treated it like a child that finds a book of matches and strikes one after another just to watch the match go up in smoke. Strategic STM is not about STM. Strategic STM is about something much bigger – something that lasts. It's about starting wildfires.

How to Start a Fire

Backpackers know that the most important part of building a fire is what you do before you strike the match. Those who brave the remote places of the earth today recognize just how crucial fire is to survival. I remember a backpacking trip years ago in the Great Smoky Mountains National Park. It was mid-winter, and snow was falling before we left the trailhead. Within an hour fresh white powder blanketed the once clearly marked path. Every opening between two trees looked like a trail. My friends and I quickly became disoriented, and soon we were lost. By late afternoon we had wandered for miles trying to find something that looked familiar. We were cold and hungry. Our water bottles were frozen inside our packs. All of our food had to be cooked. We desperately needed fire.

When we finally found our way out of the woods, to our amazement we had made a full-circle and were back at the trailhead. We quickly set up our tent. One person cleared a fire pad. Another gathered small tinder. I found some larger sticks. We took the time to meticulously build a small tee pee out of the smaller tinder and then add the larger sticks. Finally, we struck a match and prayed it would create a flame much larger than what was initially flickering. The flame began to grow, and in a matter of moments we had a blazing campfire that would bring us warmth and allow us to enjoy warm food and drink. For us, life was in the fire. We were not really in any danger. Our car was just beyond the campsite. But real backpackers don't sleep in cars. Then again, real backpackers don't camp at the trailhead. We may not have conquered the trail, but we had managed to start a fire.

The Match

The most common way to start a fire is with a match. A match, much like an STM team, has a limited amount of time with which to accomplish its intended purpose before it burns out. Most matches burn for about 5-10 seconds, and if they fail to ignite a fire on some other object that can serve as fuel, they are no longer useful. Matches are non-renewable resources, as are short-term mission ventures.

A lighted match thrown to the ground might occasionally start a significant fire, but that is not the best way to ignite a wildfire. The best way is to make the conditions right for burning by preparing a small, strategically organized gathering of kindling.

The Kindling

For the sake of the metaphor we will say that the kindling of missions is made up of indigenous national leaders on location. There is a precise way of organizing that kindling to maximize the potential for starting a raging fire. In order for STM to be strategic, there must be adequate focus on preparing the kindling in advance. e3 Partners prioritizes the equipping of indigenous leadership by going to the work area ahead of a short-term team to learn how best to serve the nationals' church planting goals. Often those leaders have no vision for church reproduction. That is why e3 Partners has made it an organizational standard to conduct a Leadership Development Conference (LDC) involving all national leaders who will be hosting the STM team. This insures that we are all in agreement that starting a wildfire through establishing rapidly reproducing indigenous churches should be the primary goal for the partnership. By conducting the LDC, e3 is in effect arranging the kindling and making the conditions right for a fire. Steffen notes, "For ongoing church planting to continue within and outside of a people group, the national leaders must own the vision, be equipped to implement it, and be given the opportunity to accomplish it successfully . . . (Church planters must) create a world vision, see it take root, train nationals to accomplish it, and delegate full responsibility to them to carry it out."[71] This is exactly the purpose of the LDC within e3 Partners' model.

The Training

In order to guard and facilitate a CPM vision, e3 Partners also orients the North American STM team prior to their arrival on the field giving them training similar to the LDC. That training focuses on the Pauline model for church planting through sessions on vision, prayer, evangelism, discipleship, gathering, leadership development, and church reproduction. These activities work together within the context of the greater goal of igniting or fueling a CPM.[72] Equipping the STM team is akin to making sure you have good matches in your matchbook. There is nothing more frustrating than trying to start a fire with wet matches, or worse, no matches at all.

Ignition

After both sides in this potential partnership have been prepared through equipping, e3 strikes the match by introducing the short-term mission team to the prepared kindling of indigenous national leadership with the shared goal of planting rapidly reproducing churches, and thereby starting a spiritual wildfire. The STM team goes into the journey with the understanding that their role is a temporary one and that their goal is to partner with the nationals in such a way as to empower them. By the time the journey comes to an end the nationals will blaze with vision, training and encouragement. Throughout the process both the STM team and the host nationals are praying that the Holy Spirit blows on the emerging flame and fans it so that many people come to Christ, become disciples, and plant new churches. At e3 Partners we have found that God answers this prayer. We have seen hundreds, sometimes thousands of people come to Christ through interdependent partnerships we call church planting campaigns. The vast majority of these new converts are the fruit of personal evangelism, and are immediately placed under the care of a trained national leader committed to establishing the new church in the target area.

Fanning the Flame

Following the catalytic event – striking the match – e3 Partners continues to partner with the indigenous leadership helping them develop national strategies. Campaigns usually result in localized fires. National strategies spread that blaze throughout the region. Indigenous church planting coaches then add fuel by equipping more and more leaders with a vision to spread the wildfire. Several of our national strategies have resulted in fires that spread across cultural barriers and even into other surrounding countries as leaders began to send teams out from their newly established churches to repeat the process, this time altogether without the help of outsiders. What God started with a

match long-since consumed can become a wildfire that
spreads a passion for His glory.

Summary of Steps toward the Strategic Use of STM

CPMs are raging throughout the world, some started or fed
at least in part by the interdependent partnership of short-
term missionaries who desire to be both obedient to
Christ's call and strategic in their purpose. The figure
below displays the four principles that guide e3 Partners'
efforts in using STM to either help start or foster CPMs.

Strategic Cross-cultural Church Planting Using STM

1. KINDLING
Arrange the kindling
through CP equipping

2. STRIKE
Strike the match through
STM CP campaigns

Striking the Match

A Metaphor for
Strategic Cross-cultural CP
using STM Teams

4. FAN
Fan the flames
through intentional
partnerships of Prayer,
Giving and Going

3. FUEL
Add more fuel
through national
strategies

e3 Partners have used the following steps to start wildfires in more than 30 countries around the globe:

Step 1: Arrange the Kindling

e3 Partners conducts a leadership development conference to equip national leaders who will host STM teams. This equipping is a biblically-based, adaptable curriculum we call *First Steps*. An overview of that curriculum will be introduced later. In order to truly prepare indigenous leaders, equipping should focus on a biblical vision for church planting achieved through strategic praying, evangelizing, disciple-making, gathering, leadership development and reproduction. Each of these concepts is taught within the context of and leading toward the goal of catalyzing a CPM. e3 Partners also prepares the STM team with these same principles so they understand their temporary role in this longer-term process and thereby maximize their impact.

Step 2: Strike the match

When both the host-receivers and the goer-guests have been equipped and oriented, we introduce the STM team for a one or two week church planting campaign. These campaigns place the ignited match of the STM team together with the arranged kindling of equipped indigenous leadership in an interdependent partnership that focuses on prayer, evangelism, discipleship and gathering of new believers, usually in an area that previously lacked a significant evangelical witness.

Recently e3 has begun to follow a strategy similar to what Jesus outlined for his disciples in Luke 10. We pair the STM teams with national leaders (and a translator if needed) and send them into an unchurched area to seek out "persons of peace."[73] After they win that person to Christ and disciple him or her, they make his or her home the focal point for the new church plant. New believers that come to faith through the campaign are then taught to gather regularly for worship and discipleship in a local home, initially led by the national church planter. Those new believers then begin to witness to their family and neighbors and all new believers are gathered. The principle here is that all the necessary resources for establishing reproducing churches are already in the harvest. Once a church is established in a given area, everything necessary for its growth and reproduction is available. Thus, as more converts are added, more fuel is gathered and the potential for its expansion increases.

Step 3: Add fuel to the fire

One of the keys for turning an STM campaign into a lasting movement is to create momentum for the indigenous church planters. e3 Partners encourages the host-receivers to make sure national workers in a given area outnumber participants in the STM team. When the guests outnumber the hosts, the work following the campaign is usually stifled by the perception that the North Americans are necessary to the on-going work of establishing churches. The purpose of the STM campaigns is to create momentum toward the establishment of reproducible churches as a part of a greater national strategy developed and driven by indigenous leadership.

A national strategy is built upon the establishment of a network of leaders (both lay and clergy) who have been equipped and mobilized to contribute to the spread of the wildfire. In order to expand this network, e3 Partners empowers and provides resources for church planting coaches who travel throughout the region conducting LDCs and national-only campaigns.[74]

Step 4: Fan the flame

After ignition has taken place and fires are burning in areas previously spiritually dry, it is important to nurture or fan those flames in such a way that they spread into the desired CPM wildfire. To do this, e3 Partners facilitates interdependent partnerships between all who have been involved in the process. Interdependent partnership means that everyone makes an investment and everyone gets a return.

e3 Partners challenges STM participants to be a part of the on-going work through monthly financial partnership with the indigenous director of the national strategy. We also challenge sending churches to recruit additional STM teams to the host area to provide additional encouragement through helping to spread the flames into other communities. All parties are informed of prayer requests from their campaign area so they can remain engaged.

Most often, however, fanning the flame becomes the job of the national church planters we initially partner with to reach a given area. As an organization, we try to encourage the national leadership during this stage of the process by providing additional training so that they can fan the flames and establish churches that reproduce.

e3 Partners' Model for Church Planting with STM Teams

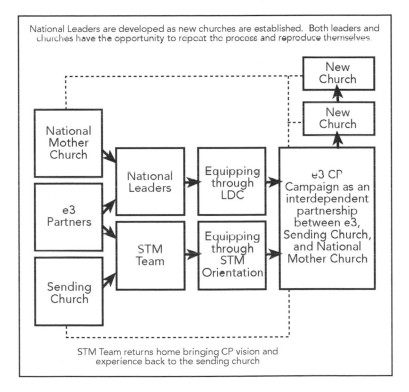

National Leaders are developed as new churches are established. Both leaders and churches have the opportunity to repeat the process and reproduce themselves.

New Church

New Church

National Mother Church

e3 Partners

Sending Church

National Leaders

STM Team

Equipping through LDC

Equipping through STM Orientation

e3 CP Campaign as an interdependent partnership between e3, Sending Church, and National Mother Church

STM Team returns home bringing CP vision and experience back to the sending church

Conclusion

The traditional distinction between the roles of clergy and laity in the work toward completion of the Great Commission has little biblical or historical warrant. Playing with matches can indeed be risky. Some feel that ordinary people should not be handling "spiritual matches" at all. The 1st century advice of Gamaliel to the Sanhedrin regarding a group of commoners (Acts 4:13 says they were uneducated and professionally untrained) may apply here. He prophesied that if the paradigm shift being ushered in by the Apostles was of human origin, it would fail. But if the movement was truly of God, it could not be overcome by all of the professional activism the Sanhedrin could muster. Why? They would be fighting against God, not man (Acts 5:33-39).

This chapter has provided a framework for how ordinary people can take part in what I believe is a movement birthed by God. God desires that all of us take part in His global plan of redemption no matter what level of training we have or what position we hold. However, He wants us to be strategic in doing so. That means making conditions right by gathering kindling, striking the match with a plan, feeding the flame by adding fuel, and asking the Holy Spirit to blow and spread the fire.

The remainder of part two is dedicated to fleshing out the principles and processes introduced here. I share these insights in hopes that both sending and receiving churches will begin to see the potential in a match and some kindling, and that wildfires can be started, filling the earth with the knowledge and glory of our LORD.

Chapter 7
Making the Conditions Right

He told them, "The harvest is plentiful, but the workers are few. Ask the Lord of the harvest, therefore, to send out workers into his harvest field. **Luke 10:2**

The Conditions are Favorable

Conditions in the southeast U.S. were right for the massive wildfire that hit my home state of Georgia this spring. With the least amount of recorded rainfall in decades, the lower part of the state became a tinderbox waiting to be ignited. In just two months a few small fires became the largest Georgia wildfire in over a century, covering more than 900 square miles, even crossing into Florida. The main locus of the fire was believed to be a power line that fell igniting the dry brush, but two teenagers were also charged with starting fires in the area.

When conditions are right, a wildfire can spread quickly. This simple fact has two implications for starting spiritual wildfires. First, spiritually dry areas are prime tinder for church planting movements. George Patterson notes that bad people provide good soil for church planting.[75] Second, fires, if uncontained, grow to impact the entire region. Both of these factors play into the goal of igniting church planting movements and thus, both are taken into consideration in e3 Partners' strategy. Conditions are indeed favorable for wildfires to ignite and spread at this time in history in many locations around the world.

Slow Down and Arrange the Kindling

Sometimes fires happen by accident, and sometimes they are set on purpose. I remember working years ago at a summer camp where we taught young boys how to start a fire with a single match. The overeager boys would often strike their match prematurely and their fires would quickly die out. We had to teach them that the success of fire-starting was determined long before the match was ignited. It was crucial that they learn to take the time to go into the woods and find tinder or kindling and then methodically arrange it in such a way that once the single match was lit, they had the greatest chance for an enduring flame. It never failed that in their enthusiasm they would try to forego the preliminary steps and strike their solitary match too soon, thereby wasting their sole catalytic resource.

Many STM teams are led by people like those boys trying to cut corners and skip crucial steps. As a result, many STMs are less than strategic, and proportionately few fires are started compared to the amount of resources consumed in their attempts. To be strategic, STM teams can't afford to skip the step of arranging the kindling.

Starting a Fire is a Process, Not an Event

Church planting is a process, not an event. In North America we often talk about organizing a launch event to start a church, but there are usually months if not years of preparation to get there. We at e3 Partners recognize that new churches are not established in a week's time. Much preparation goes into starting a new church, and much goes into growing a church to maturity. That is why we take the time to equip both the nationals and the STM team by familiarizing them with those steps.

e3 Partners' model for CP is described at length in the aforementioned First Steps curriculum that serves as the basis for equipping indigenous leadership. As we developed First Steps, our intention was that it be based upon the model of the Apostle Paul as documented in the book of Acts and described in his epistles. Paul displayed seven primary steps toward establishing new churches

(Acts 14:21-28), which have become the foundation for the e3 Partners' model. The Pauline steps are:

1. **Develop Vision** –
Multiplying Disciples that Multiply Churches

2. **Pray** –
Strategic Praying that Focuses on
Church Planting (CP)

3. **Evangelize** –
Strategic Evangelizing that Fuels CP

4. **Make Disciples** –
Strategic Discipling that Feeds CP

5. **Gather Believers** –
Strategic Gathering that Establishes
Reproducible Churches

6. **Develop Leaders** –
Strategic Equipping that Empowers CP

7. **Multiply Churches** –
Strategic Planning that Makes CP Exponential

The e3 Partners' model for CP is initially based upon interdependent partnerships between North American STM teams and national leaders, all of whom have been equipped using Paul's CP cycle as found in First Steps. The North Americans are equipped through orientation which will be detailed in the next chapter. The national leaders are equipped through a Leadership Development Conference. By using the same foundational subject matter, these two groups come to share a common vision that serves as the backdrop for a church planting campaign in an unchurched area. The goers and the hosts work together to pray, evangelize, make disciples, and gather new believers to form new churches. All the while, leaders are being developed and mother churches are multiplying. In many cases, the new churches established participate in future campaigns reproducing themselves to form third and sometimes fourth generation churches.

The Pauline Church Planting Cycle as Described in First Steps

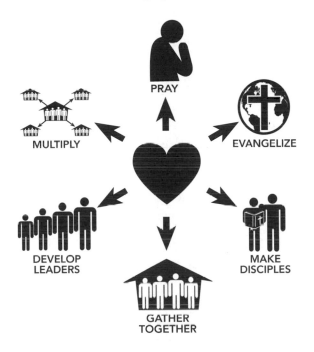

The Parable of the Harvest

In 2005 I worked with other senior staffers at e3 Partners to revise our First Steps LDC curriculum to make it more trans-culturally applicable in light of our expansion into so many different cultures. One of the things we faced was the daunting task of equipping a lay-force many of whom come from oral-based cultures where literacy is limited or absent. As we studied the model of Paul, we realized that his seven church planting principles parallel the steps in the typical agricultural cycle. Even cultures that are no longer primarily agricultural maintain a working knowledge of the harvest cycle. A parable was developed to help our staff communicate those timeless, biblical principles when training nationals and STM teams for CP. Following is a description of the parable including its biblical roots and application points.

Develop Vision

All farmers are visionaries. They look into empty fields and see a potential crop that is not yet there. It will take months of hard work driven by the motivation of seeing that vision come to fulfillment. Most farmers have days when they just do not feel like working the fields, but they do it because they know what can result if they work hard. Andy Stanley defines vision as "the difference between the way things are and the way things should be."[76] A farmer looks at an empty field – the way things are – and sees the potential harvest – the way things should be. He then acts upon that vision to make it become a reality.

Jesus taught his disciples about vision when he said in John 4:35-36, "Do you not say, 'Four months more and then the harvest'? I tell you, open your eyes and look at the fields! They are ripe for harvest." Jesus wanted his disciples to see the potential all around them. A church planter will see that potential. The Lord desires that believers join Him in the work of establishing churches in areas where there is currently little or no evangelical presence. By surveying surrounding neighborhoods and communities, church planters identify those areas that may look as if nothing is happening. The Lord wants us to see beyond what is to what can be. If we are unable to see the potential all around, we will never do the work necessary to get to the harvest. A farmer with no vision is no farmer at all. Charles Brock adds that successful church planters have, "not only the capacity to be visionaries, but the necessary discipline to pursue dreams."[77]

When it comes to church planting, vision is equivalent to seeing the potential harvest while looking at a barren field. The objective therefore is to help indigenous leaders identify areas that have little or no Gospel witness and begin plans to establish reproducing churches there.

Pray

The next principle for church planting beckons us to pray. Prayer is equivalent to breaking up the soil. After surveying the potential fields, a farmer must select a particular area of ground in which to begin his work. Most often the soil needs to be prepared or the seed will not take root.

In Matthew 13:3-8, Jesus tells us that the success of the harvest is determined by the quality of the soil in which the seed is sown. Is there something that we can do to prepare the soil so that we are guaranteed a better crop? YES! One of the most important steps in planting new churches is to prepare (through a strategic prayer effort) the area in which you will be working. Through engaging a community with a strategic prayer initiative, church planters in effect break up the hardened soil and remove stones and thorns, insuring a better return for their labor. There is also a need for continued working of the soil throughout the year to make sure nothing stands in the way of the natural growth the Lord desires to bring.

The Lord desires that believers join Him in this work by praying for the people to whom they will be ministering. Patterson notes, "Church reproduction is supernatural, so prayer is always part of it; God enables churches to multiply in response to our requests."[78] Garrison adds, "Only when prayer comes to characterize the life of the missionaries and church planters, does it spread to their team members and to those they are trying to reach."[79] By getting out into the community and establishing prayer points or engaging in prayer walking, church planters become aware of areas that need to be broken up through prayer. We have observed that planting a church without first breaking up the soil through prayer means very little will take root and grow. Thus, the objective when training church planters in prayer is to help them identify needs and pray specifically for the harvest field in order to plow up the hardened spiritual ground.

Evangelize

Evangelism is equivalent to sowing the seed. Once a farmer selects the area he intends to farm and breaks up the soil, he scatters the seed plentifully. He understands that in order to see a bountiful harvest he must sow more than enough seed, for not all seed will take root. The Apostle Paul taught the Corinthian Church this principle in 2 Corinthians 9:6; "Remember this: Whoever sows sparingly will also reap sparingly, and whoever sows generously will also reap generously." Paul was talking about sowing financially, but the principle applies here as well. When people put much seed into good soil, they can expect a great harvest. However, when only a few seeds are put out, a small harvest can be expected. In order to establish a church we need to sow the seed of the Gospel in abundance. The more seed sown – the more the Gospel is presented – the more people we are likely to see come to faith in Christ through the sovereign work of the Holy Spirit.

The objective when training church planters is to help them engage the harvest field through evangelistic efforts. By getting out into the community and sharing the Gospel through relationships, believers are in effect sowing spiritual seed in expectation of a great harvest. If we try to plant a church without sowing the seed abundantly through evangelistic outreach, we will reap sparingly. Garrison again adds, "Essential to every movement is the principle of over-sowing . . . In CPMs we find hundreds and thousands of people hearing the Gospel every day and out of this abundant sowing, a growing harvest begins to take place."[80]

Make Disciples

Making disciples is equivalent to nurturing the new growth. The most crucial time in the lifespan of a plant is just after the seed comes to life and breaks through the soil into the harsh conditions of the outside world. Because the tiny plant has shallow roots it is particularly susceptible to a number of factors that could kill it before it grows into maturity. For example, if the sun shines directly on the plant and its roots cannot take in enough moisture, the plant will wither and die. Or if a heavy rain comes and washes the topsoil away, the small plant will be uprooted, also resulting in death. But if the tiny plant is nurtured in its early stages of life and is given the opportunity to establish deep roots, it will continue to grow to maturity.

As disciple-makers we can learn a great deal from this parable. After people come to faith in Christ, like a new plant, they are faced with many challenges. Because they have no spiritual roots, new believers are particularly susceptible to the challenges that life brings. Jesus taught this very thing in Matthew 13:23: "But the one who received the seed that fell on good soil is the man who hears the word and understands it. He produces a crop, yielding a hundred, sixty or thirty times what was sown." The difference between spiritual death and vibrant, reproducing spiritual life is found in understanding the Word of God. We must be careful to nurture the growth of new believers through discipleship. Investing time and energy into new believers, we are cultivating hearts in such a way as to maximize their potential to reproduce and bring forth a greater harvest.

The Lord desires church planters to join Him in the work of making disciples by establishing people in a proper understanding of His Word. Discipleship is as much about nurturing relationships as it is about information.[81] If we try to plant a church without taking the time to establish discipling relationships with new believers, we will find that the harsh conditions of life will prevent them from taking root. Therefore, the objective when training church planters is that they learn to make disciples that love and obey Christ.

Gather Together

We establish churches by gathering disciples together for worship and fellowship. This is equivalent to bringing in the crops. The day when all his work culminates in a great harvest is the most joyful time for a farmer. This is the day he envisioned from the start. This is the day that motivated all the hard labor. As much work as the farmer has done, he understands that all he did was make the conditions right for growth. There is no question that God is the Lord of the Harvest. In many respects, a farmer is merely a steward of God's work. And because of that, a farmer knows how crucial harvest day is. If the harvest is left in the field too long it will spoil. It is vitally important to bring in the harvest while it is ripe. Jesus taught His disciples about this when he said in Mark 4:26-29,

> *"This is what the kingdom of God is like. A man scatters seed on the ground. Night and day, whether he sleeps or gets up, the seed sprouts and grows, though he does not know how. All by itself the soil produces grain - first the stalk, then the head, then the full kernel in the head. As soon as the grain is ripe, he puts the sickle to it, because the harvest has come."*

The time to harvest is as soon as the grain is ripe. Any delay is poor stewardship. The Lord desires that church planters join Him in the work of gathering the harvest through establishing new churches. A storehouse is a place where the crops will be kept and remain useful. By establishing new churches we are in effect forming storehouses that will cause the harvest to last. If we sow seed through evangelistic outreach without bringing the new believers into the storehouse, they will quickly fall away and will be spiritually unusable.

This leads us to an important question: Can a church be established through an STM team in just a week? Probably not. Meece observes that short-term teams, "may start (churches), but the infant churches wither without adequate discipling".[82] This is precisely why it is imperative to work through existing indigenous churches when at all possible in order to help them reproduce new

churches. e3 Partners' senior staffer Sam Ingrassia
speaks about church planting in terms of conception,
pregnancy and birth. He notes that because we utilize
the mother-church model for church planting in most of
our partnerships, we enter the process at different points
in each location. Some churches have no vision at all for
church planting so our equipping and short-term teams
help them to "conceive." Other host churches have the
vision, and have already started working toward it, and
we enter in the pregnancy phase to help with development. Many times conception and pregnancy have taken
place and our teams arrive for the birth. Building on this
analogy I often think of myself as a mid-wife rather than
a church planter.

R. Bruce Carlton notes, "Few, if any, indigenous
CPMs have been born out of or sustained by the efforts
of outsiders who sought to control the planting of new
groups."[83] This indicates that neither short-term nor long-
term missionaries are really able to establish new churches. It can only be done through interdependent partnership with equipped and empowered nationals.

Develop Leaders

Developing new indigenous leaders is equivalent to gathering the seed for a future harvest.[84] Every farmer understands that the key to next year's crop is found within
this year's harvest – the seed for future sowing.
Therefore, we could say that the resources are within the
harvest! The same is true when it comes to planting

churches. The key to future church plants are found in this first harvest. Jesus spoke about this in John 12:24, "I tell you the truth, unless a kernel of wheat falls to the ground and dies, it remains only a single seed. But if it dies, it produces many seeds." If we as leaders die to ourselves and begin to invest in other new leaders, we will multiply our vision and influence, and in effect expand the Kingdom of God through an army of church planters. The best way of doing that is through on-the-job training – giving new disciples responsibilities in the church and training them so they can eventually lead a church themselves. This takes humility on the part of a church planter. Paul understood this when he wrote in 1 Corinthians 3:6-9, "I planted the seed, Apollos watered it, but God made it grow. So neither he who plants nor he who waters is anything, but only God, who makes things grow. The man who plants and the man who waters have one purpose, and each will be rewarded according to his own labor. For we are God's fellow workers; you are God's field." Establishing new churches requires multiple leaders – a team of sorts. Where do we find these leaders? We will find them within the harvest.

The Lord desires that church planters join Him in the work of developing new leaders who will in turn reproduce. Within every seed there is the potential of millions more seeds. But the key to getting the millions is found in the one seed doing what it was created for – reproduction! The objective in developing leaders is that they learn to reproduce themselves by mentoring newer leaders that will carry on the day to day functions of the church. By developing new leaders within the harvest, we are in effect gathering the seeds of reproduction that will result in future harvests and more new churches. Planting new churches without developing new leaders limits growth potential and in effect prevents future church plants.

Multiply Churches

Multiplying churches is equivalent to expanding the harvest field. In Mark 4, Jesus taught the disciples using a parable about a farmer. Every farmer wants to see a harvest, but he knows it will not come easily. It is the end-vision of the harvest that gets him into the fields in the first place. He can see in his mind what is yet to become reality. Before he plants a single seed, he sees the potential of a hillside covered with crops full of life. And so the farmer goes into an empty field covered with stones and begins to work. First he breaks up the hardened soil so when he begins to sow the seed, it will penetrate and take root. Next he takes the seed and begins to scatter it over the prepared ground. Then he waits for what only God can do – bring forth life from a dead seed. When tiny plants break the surface of the ground the farmer nurtures the growth by removing weeds, providing adequate water, and keeping out birds and vermin. He realizes that already these plants have the potential for reproduction within themselves if only he can nurture them to bear fruit. After they establish strong roots and reach maturity, the farmer goes into the field and begins to harvest, gathering the fruit into his storehouse. There he meticulously preserves the seed for his next planting season, for the resources are found within the harvest. And so his vision enlarges because now he has even more seed to sow. The process starts all over again only now he has to plow up new ground and expand the harvest. Any good farmer knows if he plants the same crop in the same field year after year the soil will be ruined and nothing will grow there.

The objective when training church planters in multiplication is to instill within the new churches the vision and priority to reproduce. Garrison has found that, "CPMs did not emerge without a deliberate commitment to plant reproducing churches."[85] I remember once conducting an LDC in South Asia. After the final session one young church planter raised his hand enthusiastically declaring, "In our land we harvest the crops three times each year! So we will make it our goal for churches to reproduce at least three times each year." I appreciated his vision, and I believe that it is through leaders like him that church planting movements are kindled.

Lecture + Lab = Learning

Developing leaders with a vision and skills to kindle or spread a CPM is a multi-faceted task. Leaders are not developed through courses or seminars alone, but through a combination of teaching buttressed with much practical experience. For this reason, e3 Partners balance our approach to leadership development by using complimentary approaches.

e3 International Director Mike Jorgensen uses the analogy that in chemistry if a person only sits through lectures and never applies what they have learned, everything remains theoretical and advancement is prohibited for lack of practice. But if a person goes directly to the lab and fails to get the background for the subject through lecture, the results can be disastrous! Learning is balanced when students attend lecture and then apply what they heard through laboratory exercises.

We develop national leaders using this same approach. We begin by taking them through the fundamentals of church planting at our LDC. This conference walks the leaders through the biblical vision for church planting followed by the first steps to actually establishing a reproducing church. We do not simply teach at the conference, but instead we facilitate group discussion and planning. Most importantly, we try to go out and practice immediately following various sessions to give those in attendance a laboratory in which to test and practice what they are learning. For example, following the session on evangelism, we actually take the group into a neighborhood where they practice what they have learned by sharing the Gospel using a tool called the Evangecube

93

(*www.e3resources.org*) and their personal testimony. After the session on gathering believers into a house church, we have them break into small groups and practice, or if possible gather converts that were won to faith during the Evangelism lab exercise. Subsequent to the LDC, these leaders begin to implement what they have learned by going out and reproducing the teaching in the mother churches and in the neighborhoods they are targeting for new church plants. This balanced approach facilitates the rapid implementation and reproduction of new churches.

A Big Fire and a Plentiful Harvest

Conditions must be right for a wildfire to ignite and spread. The same can be said of a CPM. We have outlined several steps to establishing new reproducing indigenous churches using STM teams as catalysts. We looked at Paul's example as described in our First Steps curriculum. We saw that by understanding the harvest cycle anyone can contribute strategically to the process. It all starts with God's vision spreading among the laborers. Vision gives birth to prayer as we work together to break up the hardened ground. Then we sow the seed of the Gospel through evangelism, remembering that if we sow plentifully, we will reap plentifully. When people come to faith, we nurture them until they are rooted in the faith, all the while understanding that they already have what it takes to reproduce. If we leave the crops in the field too long they go bad, so we bring in the harvest forming new churches. Within those churches are leaders that provide the seed for the next harvest. We identify those leaders and begin to give them on-the-job training. Then we go out into the ever-widening harvest field and begin again. In fact, we may have multiple crops going in multiple fields all at once.

Whether talking about the spread of crops, wildfires, or CPMs, the principles remain the same. The conditions must be right for any of these to spread quickly. You can be a part of a movement of God when you take time to make the conditions right.

Striking the Match

Chapter 8

Striking the Match

Consider what a great forest is set on fire by a small spark.

James 3:5

The Problem with Wet Matches

Have you ever tried to start a fire using wet matches? It is next to impossible. The same can be said of trying to ignite a CPM with an STM team that is unprepared. The key to strategic short-term involvement is in orienting the team toward the over-arching purpose of the journey. When there are no clearly defined goals it is easy to wander into the previously discussed pitfalls. However, when the vision for a rapidly reproducing indigenous church planting movement is the core tool for recruiting and the basis for all orientation, being strategic is a natural outflow. In preparing STM teams I try to communicate to participants that their role is like that of a match – to serve the long-term goal of starting a "wildfire" while understanding that we are personally expendable in the process.

Who's to Blame?

STM is certainly not without its pitfalls. Unfortunately, often little is done to ensure that short-term trips are strategic in nature. Most trips today are more tourism and personal fulfillment than strategy and fulfillment of the Great Commission. David Garrison asserts in his booklet called Church Planting Movements:

> *The key to effective use of volunteers in missions is orientation. Most short-term volunteers want to be strategic, but don't realize that some forms of help can actually hinder a Church Planting Movement...*
> *Constructing church buildings, subsidizing pastors and creating dependency are well-intentioned obstacles to a Church Planting Movement.*[86]

If what Garrison says about volunteers wanting to be strategic is true, then the pitfalls to STM are emerging in the orientation and use of such groups, which places the responsibility back on the sending entity who organizes the journey. An army of volunteers are waiting to help fulfill the Great Commission if only someone will orient them in how to do that strategically. "The church should use all means at its disposal to make sure this is taking place."[87] How can the pitfalls be minimized so that ordinary people come in line with God's plan, and in His power, help to complete the Great Commission?

Orientation for Strategic STM

Orientation for most mission trips is limited to packing lists and general cultural information. I usually start by defining clearly the roles the team will play in the greater context of what is already happening among their national hosts. In order to facilitate the type of interdependence that results in strategic STM, care must be taken to orient the STM participants far in advance of the journey. This is crucial because host-receivers often pick up on the practices that are brought in by outsiders. If we fail to model a biblical approach to church planting, the very people we are trying to help may actually acquire our bad habits, hindering the entire process.

Following is an outline to help orient North Americans for participation in a short-term church planting campaign:

First Meeting: Partnering for Long-term Impact
    1. **Church Planting Orientation**
        A. Developing Vision –
            Multiplying Disciples that Multiply Churches
            ▲ Highlighting the Book of Acts and the model of Paul as our lead in establishing reproducing churches.
        B. Pray – Strategic Praying that Focuses on CP
            ▲ Equipping to prayer walk and establish "Lighthouses of Prayer" in areas where there is no evangelical church.

C. **Evangelize** –
Strategic Evangelizing that Fuels CP
▲ Equipping to use the Evangecube or other contextualized approach to sharing the Gospel in the host culture.

D. **Make Disciples** –
Strategic Discipling that Fuels CP
▲ Equipping in biblical disciple-making principles and introduction to contextualized methods and curriculums that could be used to facilitate discipleship among new believers.[88]

E. **Gather Believers** – Strategic Gathering that Establishes Reproducible Churches
▲ The Biblical Nature of the Church
▲ Modeling the Biblical Church[89]

F. **Develop Leaders** –
Strategic Equipping that Empowers CP
▲ A look at biblical examples of good leaders and bad leaders and how to develop good ones.

G. **Multiply Churches** –
Strategic Planning that Makes CP Exponential
▲ Equipping with an evaluative tool that I developed called the Acts Strategy Matrix in order to find and fill the weaknesses in a church's missions strategy. **(See Appendix One)**

Second Meeting: Context and Cross-Cultural Communication

2. **Cultural Orientation**
   A. **Country-specific Information** –
      an overview of the country's history and development, stats, etc. for greater understanding of the context that has shaped the thinking of those whom we will work with.
   B. **Area-specific Information** – equips the team for a greater understanding of the particular area where we will be focusing.
   C. **Worldview-specific Information** – includes overview of religious beliefs and practices and ways to effectively communicate the Gospel in that context.
   D. **Language-specific Information** – entry level training on phrases that will be helpful at bridging the cultural divide, as well as guidelines for using an interpreter.
   E. **Basic Principles of Cross-cultural Communication** – overview of the "signal systems" to provide the framework for understanding and communication across cultural barriers.[90]
   F. **Minimizing Culture Shock**

Third Meeting: Spiritual and Logistical Preparation

3. **Spiritual and Logistical Orientation**
   A. Review Principles from Orientation 1 & 2
   B. Review pertinent logistics information
   C. How This STM Journey Fits into a Comprehensive Long-term CP Strategy

▲ Overview the national-composed CP strategy and how this team can contribute to that strategy in a way resulting in lasting impact.

D. Spiritual preparation – devotionals, prayer and worship

A Typical e3 Partners Campaign

After the kindling has been arranged and the match has been prepared, it is time for ignition. A typical e3 Partners' church planting campaign has several core elements that make it trans-culturally applicable in most settings where there is a host mother church.[91]

The first day of the campaign is usually devoted to introducing the STM team to their national hosts for a collaborative orientation. I like to keep things simple for my teams so I give them one or two key words to remember that are the foundation for each day on the field. This first day's keywords are "relationships" and "prayer." It is crucial that the STM team take the time to get to know those they will be working alongside. They need to learn about not only the hosts, but also the area in which they will be working. Often this orientation takes place at the mother church(es) so that the STM team can get a vision for what the host church is trying to reproduce. Later in the day teams go into target neighborhoods and begin prayer walking together.

On the second day of the campaign the STM team and the national team travel together to the target area and

divide up into teams of 2-3 persons and begin to go house
to house looking for opportunities to share the Gospel.
The keywords for day 2 are "pray" and "evangelize." Each
team is usually composed of a national host, a STM team
member, and a translator. Before the group approaches a
home they delegate various responsibilities between
them. One person shares a personal testimony of how he
or she came to faith in Jesus and the other uses the
Evangecube and the Bible to share a simple and clear
Gospel presentation. Each person prays while the other
is engaged with listeners. Whether the listeners choose
to surrender to Christ or not, they are invited to an
evening home meeting within walking distance of where
they live. National hosts usually designate this home
prior to the arrival of the STM team. After a full day of
these teams going through a neighborhood, they make
their way to the location for the evening home meeting.
Each night they conduct this meeting with new believers
and seekers using a simple and reproducible format in
hopes that a new church will be birthed in their midst.

On the next several days of the campaign there is a
shift in focus and the keywords become "make disciples"
and "evangelize." I emphasize that the Great
Commission tells us to make disciples, not just converts.
Therefore, the teams focus on going back to the homes of
those that have shown interest and the discipleship
process begins. The great thing about doing this in an
unchurched target area is that every new believer has a

massive network of lost family and friends we can help them reach out to with the same Gospel they have just embraced. By shifting our evangelistic focus to the networks of new believers, the new church is able to develop organically along the lines of already established relationships. The evening meetings continue throughout the week as these networks are introduced to one another creating a growth momentum.

On the final few days of the campaign the STM team steps further back so the existing momentum is not be tied to their presence. The keywords become "empower" and "encourage." The goal is to empower the national leadership and the new church as they prepare to repeat the Pauline cycle of developing vision, praying, evangelizing, making disciples, gathering together, developing leaders and multiplying.

Starting with the End in Sight

The contextualized leadership development principles we use have been dubbed "M.A.W.L.," or "Model, Assist, Watch, then Leave."[92] We equip our STM teams in these principles in anticipation of the church planting campaign. When the equipped teams arrive they are partnered with national leaders for the outreach, and over the course of the week they model prayer, evangelism, discipleship and gathering. After a few days of modeling, the STM team shifts gears and focuses primarily on assisting the nationals in doing these tasks. By the end of the campaign the ministry has been completely transferred to the national leadership and the STM team watches the hosts at work, and then leaves them behind better equipped for establishing churches.

Sometimes we find that the MAWL process actually flows from the nationals to the STM team. It is obvious that nationals will know the most contextualized approach to reaching their own people with the Gospel and establishing churches among them. Some might argue that STM teams are a waste because they can not possibly do these tasks as effectively as nationals. One of the most important things that the STM team brings is encouragement. The STM team acts as a catalyst to get the nationals into the unreached areas and as a result, more churches are established, not necessarily because of the prowess of the amateur STM participants, but because of the encouragement they brought to the national leaders. We have even found that many times STM teams take what they have learned from their national partners and apply it back home in their own churches, resulting in the desired interdependent partnership. One of the greatest things about the MAWL approach is that the indigenous national leaders can then repeat that process in each area they work (with or without North American STM teams) resulting in a potentially exponential number of equipped national leaders, which is a necessity for any CPM to ignite or thrive.

When It's Done Right

In conclusion, using STM teams to ignite or contribute to CPMs can be very effective if care is taken to adequately equip both sides beforehand. We never want to create dependency between the new churches and the STM teams, so we work to prepare both parties ahead of time for this interdependent partnership. Over the course of the campaign we constantly remind the North Americans that they are to equip and encourage the nationals in such a way that we work ourselves out of a job by transferring the work completely to the nationals. By doing this, time and time again we have seen these new churches reproducing on their own – sometimes multiple times – within a short period following a campaign. Thus, these STM teams have been used by God to fuel and sometimes even ignite emerging wildfires around the globe.

Chapter 9
The Real Pro Pyros

"The priests are to put fire on the altar and arrange wood on the fire" **Leviticus 1:7**

They Know What They're Doing

Pyromania is an irresistible urge to set things ablaze. I remember as a child being mesmerized by flames dancing in a campfire. I thought I knew something about fire until I was burned playing around with it. It only took a split second to realize my fascination with fire could be dangerous if not coupled with knowledge and wisdom.

While I have asserted up to this point that missions is not for professionals alone, I believe there are some pros we all should be paying attention to. We need to listen to the real professionals. Not those that just sit around and study fires. I'm talking about the indigenous national Christians who want more than you or I to see the Gospel ablaze in their culture. Those are the real pro pyros.

In this chapter we give a voice to the indigenous leaders who have hosted e3 Partners' STM teams. What they have to say is crucial in determining how we should best strategize. The first part of this section is based upon quantitative research (statistics) conducted on nationals, both clergy and laity, who worked in partnership on an e3 Partners' STM church planting campaign. The second part is based upon qualitative research (interview-style) conducted on national leaders that work with e3 Partners to coordinate on-going church planting efforts in their countries. Together, these two research methodologies provide keen insight into how the nationals feel about and are impacted by the type of STM work that is central to the e3 Partners' model.[93] What you will read here however, is not just applicable to the ministry of e3 Partners. You will hear the voices of literally hundreds of national host-receivers about how any STM team can become more effective. Senders and goers alike need to hear and heed these voices.

Listening to the Pros
through Quantitative Research

In 2006 I developed a 26-question survey that was based around the Pauline Cycle for church planting as detailed earlier in chapter 7. The survey was designed to measure

changes among indigenous national hosts in their attitude, behavior, and activities with regards to church
planting. We gave the survey to nearly one hundred
nationals in three different countries before the LDC (pre-
test), then again before the STM campaign (mid-test), and
once more after the STM campaign (post-test).[94] By comparing responses from everyone who completed the pre
and mid-tests, I was able to isolate the variable of e3
Partners' equipping LDCs and determine how that training impacted understanding and application of CP principles among participants. By comparing responses from
everyone who completed the mid and post-tests, I was
able to isolate the variable of e3 Partners' STM team
presence and determine how working alongside North
Americans impacted their understanding and application
of CP principles. Finally, by comparing responses from
everyone who completed the pre and post-tests I was able
to determine how participation in the entire e3 model
(both the LDC and STM campaign) collectively impacted
their understanding and application of CP principles.
This group will hereafter be referred to as the experimen-
tal group (EG).

In addition, I also conducted research on a control
group (CG) made up of 42 Peruvian nationals who have
taken the e3 model and made it their own. It should be
noted that all the members of this group had participated
in the e3 church planting model by hosting and working
alongside a North American STM team at some time in the

past. Under the direction of the Peruvian national director they started running national-only campaigns several years ago where they participate in their own LDC training and then run STM campaigns where clergy and laity from one area are mobilized to work in another city (and sometimes country) to assist mother churches in starting new congregations. The members of the CG used all the same tools from e3 Partners (the Evangecube, the e3 tract and the First Steps manual) with the only difference being that no North American STM team participated. These 42 respondents of the CG completed both a pre and post-test providing statistical representation of the e3 model with no North Americans, as well as providing a control group against which those in the EG were compared.

Summary of Quantitative Findings

Following is a complete summary of the relationships that were established as statistically significant.[95]

Relationships were established between participation in the e3 LDC and the following:

- increase in the number of nationals participating in personal and corporate prayer for CP
- increase among nationals in evangelistic outreach through personal testimonies and Gospel presentations
- increase in evangelistic harvest among some of the nationals
- increase in the number of nationals meeting with new believers to disciple them

- increase in the number of nationals gathering new believers for worship
- increase in the number of nationals leading in CP activities

Relationships were established between hosting and working alongside the North American e3 STM team during a church planting campaign and the following:

- increase in the number of national laity viewing themselves as evangelists
- increased effort among nationals praying for the lost around them
- increase in the net number of nationals presenting the Gospel and net number of Gospel presentations
- increase in the number of nationals sharing their personal testimony and in the frequency of their sharing
- increase in the number of nationals experiencing an evangelistic harvest and an increase in net professions of faith (POFs)
- increase in the net number of nationals gathering new believers for worship and in the frequency of their gatherings
- increase in the net number of nationals serving as leaders in CP activities

Relationships were established between participation in the complete e3 church planting model (LDC+ STM campaign) and the following:

- increase in the frequency of nationals gathering to pray about starting a new church

- increase in the frequency of nationals sharing the Gospel with unbelievers
- increase in the frequency of nationals sharing their personal testimony with unbelievers
- increase in the number of persons led to faith in Jesus Christ through a personal Gospel presentation
- increase in the frequency of nationals gathering new believers for worship in small groups or churches
- increase in the frequency of nationals serving as leaders of small groups and outreach efforts

Relationships were established between groups (EG and CG) as a result of participation in the e3 church planting campaign with respect to the following:

- the frequency with which nationals share their personal testimony with the CG showing a greater frequency
- the number of people led to faith in Jesus Christ through a personal Gospel presentation with the CG seeing a greater harvest
- the frequency of meeting to disciple new believers with the CG showing a higher frequency
- the frequency of gathering new believers together for worship with the CG showing a higher frequency
- the interest level in helping to plant new churches with the CG showing a greater interest
- the reproducibility of the model as seen in national-only campaigns (CG) which proved even more effective than campaigns involving North American STM teams (EG) on many items

At first glance, this information may seem to indicate that nationals do better without North American STM teams. The reality is, however, that every member of the control group had participated in hosting one or more e3 Partners STM teams in the past. Learning from those campaigns, nationals reproduced and indigenized the model so they became goer-guests being hosted by inexperienced churches within their counties. Thus statistical relationships actually serve to verify what can happen in the lives of nationals that host strategic STM teams. They improved on what they experienced to the point that they no longer need an external catalyst for church planting because they have become the catalysts.

Summary

My purpose in attempting to identify relationships between participation in the e3 model and changes in CP understanding, attitudes and activities among nationals, is to evaluate statistically whether or not STM is being used in a strategic manner by e3 Partners. If such a relationship could be established statistically, then STM, at least in the case of e3 Partners, could be deemed a valid model for using STM teams because of their contributions to longer-term strategy of helping nationals establish new indigenous churches. The research shows that in most cases there is a positive relationship in clarifying and catalyzing CP understanding, attitudes, and activities for those nationals who participate in the e3 model.

Listening to the Pros through Qualitative Research[96]

The qualitative surveys that provide the information contained in this part of the chapter were conducted in order to glean the perspective of those indigenous National Directors (ND) whose work with e3 Partners is of a more permanent and comprehensive nature. There were four respondents each from Africa, Eastern Europe, and Latin America, two from India and one from the Middle East. The various regions represented help to provide a more trans-cultural understanding of the ministry of e3 Partners and the effects of its use of STM in CP work.

Evaluating e3 Partners' Equipping Conferences

Because equipping is central to the e3 Partners' model, I asked the national leaders from each country to explain in what ways LDCs have been either helpful or harmful in the planting of churches in their respective areas. Every respondent unanimously stated the LDC was crucial to the establishment of CP vision among national pastors and lay leaders. Almost as emphatic was the declaration that LDCs do in fact equip leaders with the tools necessary to establish new churches. One Latin American leader noted that, "LDCs have provided practical help in the steps necessary to start new churches . . . and have helped pastors to look beyond their own little flock and be aware that there are people all around them without a saving relationship with Christ." In addition, several national leaders stated that one of the greatest values of the LDC is that it is simple and helpful at mobilizing their laity to get involved in CP work. If wildfires are going to be started around the world it will be because the kindling has been made ready providing fuel for the fire. According to our national hosts, the e3 Partners' LDC is effective in doing just that.

Evaluating the STM Campaigns

Along with the LDC, the STM Campaign is another key component in the e3 Partners' CP model. Thus, the national leaders were asked to describe in what ways the STM Campaigns have been helpful or harmful in the planting of churches in their respective areas. One of the most interesting responses was given by four different leaders – that the North American is like "bait" that gets the attention of the lost in their communities. This novelty factor is by no means universal with the rise of anti-American sentiment sweeping the globe today. However, it should be noted that many doors are opened to the foreign guest that may not have been opened otherwise when it comes to engaging an unchurched area with the Gospel.

Another positive aspect of the STM Campaign was described variously as initiative, momentum, and motivation. All three of these terms indicate that something either latent or altogether lacking (namely CP activity) was set into motion upon the arrival of the North American STM team. A benefit of this motivation comes

from the fact that many of the STMers are lay persons
and this is highly motivating for the national laity as they
see that they too can be engaged in the CP process. One
of e3 Partners' African leaders noted the simple presence
of the STMer "speaks volumes of love" to both the national hosts and those whom they are reaching out among.
Other national leaders mentioned that STMers often
model a godly lifestyle, evangelistic zeal, unity in the
faith, generosity, and organizational skills. One said
being around these teams he and his people are able to
see "living Christianity." Another leader adds that the
most encouraging aspect is that the STM teams are usually comprised primarily of lay people who sacrifice time,
money and the comforts of home to help them reach their
neighbors.

As for negative factors mentioned, all of the usual
things showed up on the list: paternalism, dependency,
cultural insensitivity, communication problems, lack of
flexibility, cost-benefit ratio, and a vacation mentality.
Several national leaders noted that they had worked with
other STM sending entities before e3 Partners and that
many of these negatives have been proportionately less
pervasive when hosting e3 Partners' Campaigns. This is
not to say that e3 Partners has not had its share of culturally insensitive, inflexible, vacationing philanthropists
on our campaigns. We would be naïve to think that these
things are not happening. The key, however, is to know
and understand the potential for these negative factors

and to create environments that lessen the likelihood of their occurrence.

As a general rule, all e3 Partners' Church Planters orient their STM teams long before leaving the US. One of the topics of discussion deals with finances. All STMers are told they are never to give gifts or finances except through the approval of our host National Director who will evaluate whether or not the need is legitimate and if meeting it would be beneficial toward the goal of planting reproducing churches. By and large this method of orientation has been effective, but there are occasional STMers that ignore guidelines and give secretly, often causing great harm in the wake of their generosity. I sometimes collect all cash from my STMers before we leave, put it into envelopes labeled with the owners' names, and have them come to me when they need money. Although this may seem a bit militant, it has been effective. You can't spend what you don't have.

Another potentially negative factor mentioned is that national pastors sometimes view STM teams as workers who replace their own laity on a job rather than supplement them. For the most part, however, the national leaders reported that if anything, the presence of the STM team brings out more of their people to work in the CP process. When orienting the national host pastors at the LDCs, e3 Partners makes it clear there should be several national lay workers on the campaign for every North American. In this way, the work is not viewed as being tied to the presence of a foreigner. Occasionally STM teams must be diverted away from partnering with a national church when the host pastor has failed to mobilize his own laity for a campaign.

Best Aspects of the e3 Partners' Church Planting Model

When asked what is the best aspect of e3 Partners' CP model, respondents listed characteristics such as lay involvement, focus on indigenous leadership, empowering partnerships, reproducibility by nationals, and a solid biblical basis. Interestingly, the idea that e3 Partners empowers nationals to establish indigenous churches spanned all four geographical regions that were surveyed. In relation to e3 Partners' CP model the word "simple" was used no less than five times. One leader warned, however, "There needs to be more recognition that e3 Partners does not have a monopoly on the best method to reach people and plant churches. In the past they have been open to receiving suggestions based on field experience, and I hope they continue that way. There is the danger that the method will get set in concrete." This exhortation from our national brother is taken to heart. Anyone involved in leading STM teams needs to heed the advice of our national partners and constantly ask for honest and reflective feedback, for they are the ones that truly understand what is happening on the ground and how to start fires there.

Aspects of the e3 Partners' Church Planting Model that Need Improvement

When asked what elements of e3's CP model needs improvement, respondents were gracious but honest. The most significant and trans-cultural comment was that in order to truly establish churches e3 Partners should always extend its focus longer than just a single STM campaign in a given area. Many of our national leaders mentioned that e3 Partners should consider ways to build more lasting relationships with the individual churches that they have helped to plant. One African leader warned that our approach not be a "hit and run exercise" where one week there is an e3 Partners presence and the next week that presence is gone, never to return. An Eastern European leader added, "To start a new church and to develop a relationship with the people we need to go to the same locations two or three years (in a row)." Another from that region attributed the sometimes ineffective follow-up to e3 Partners' failure to keep in touch with the pastors and local leaders with whom they have worked.

The Need to Facilitate Longer-term Partnerships

Several national leaders expressed the desire to create sustainable relationships between STM sending churches and the churches they helped to plant. One national leader set forth a detailed plan to cut the number of STMers going to a village each year while increasing the number of nationals as a means for solidifying the relationship to the focus area. Another national leader emphasized that churches in the US should not just send STM teams, but should rather use that as a platform for adopting an unreached people in his homeland planning for a ten-to-twenty-year partnership with establishing a CPM among that people as the common goal.

In defense of e3 Partners, we have chosen to use the "mother church model" for CP because we recognize it is not likely that North Americans will be able to remain in a close enough relationship to a national church over time.[97] All these national leaders have been recruited and trained with that understanding, and yet one stated, "I know you consider that this responsibility (follow-up and growing a new church to maturity) is up to the local church, but from my understanding this segment (estab-lishing a lasting relationship) is important for e3 Partners to consider."

There are North American churches that have caught this vision and maximized their impact. New Hope Baptist Church in San Diego, CA traveled with e3 Mission Director Dan Hitzhusen to northeast India over a decade ago and went on to adopt an unreached people there known as the Meitei. Over the course of the last decade New Hope has sent many teams to work alongside the nationals helping them establish dozens of churches. The result is that today there is a viable movement of indigenously reproducing churches. Pastor Joe Rhodes at New Hope has seen firsthand what God can do when strategic short-term mission teams are a significant part of a long-term strategy. Potomac Heights Baptist Church located in Indian Head, Maryland is another that has made it a point to focus on the depth of their relationship with host-receivers in Bolivia. As a result, this church of around 200 people has emphasized prayer for their Bolivian partners and has mobilized ten percent of their congregation to go on a church planting campaign in the last few years. Pastor Gary Willet has learned there is fruit on both sides of that interdependent relationship. These success stories are just a few examples of efforts on the part of e3 in response to the suggestions of our national hosts.

Be Flexible

Regarding the tools used in e3 Partners' STM campaigns, one national leader advised us not to be too rigid about the use of the e3 Tract.[98] Coming from a former Soviet area, he reminded e3 Partners that people are very skeptical about giving out too much personal information for fear that it would be misused. He noted that in his country the Evangecube and a person's testimony should be emphasized over the tract. On the other hand, several leaders from Latin America mentioned they felt e3 Partners was becoming too focused on the Evangecube, questioning both the reproducibility and the consistency of the message when that tool is used. One of those leaders noted, "The tract is much more reproducible and available and includes some facts that are not as directly covered in most Cube (Evangecube) presentations . . . The tract also lends itself to dialogue with people (rather than monologue with regard to the Evangecube)." Over the last few years e3 Partners has been addressing this issue through the development of its national strategies wherein national leaders inform us which tools are most appropriate and effective in their areas.

One national leader said, "The e3 Partners' model is not just focused on evangelism but emphasizes the steps that should follow evangelism through to starting a new church." Another lamented his past involvement with some LTM personnel and contrasted his experiences with e3 Partners by noting, "e3 came to *do* (emphasis his), not just talk about mission."

Suggested Changes to the e3 Model

When asked what they would change about the e3 Partners CP model, a few respondents replied they would not change anything. Interestingly, most were national leaders with the shortest history with e3 Partners and still in a "honeymoon period," or they may fear their responses might not be kept in confidence and thereby jeopardize their ministry position. Among those who gave a thoughtful response, several mentioned there could be even better equipping of the STM team prior to arrival on the field so they have a more accurate understanding of the culture enabling them to be more effective in their short tenure.

One African leader said e3 Partners should trust its national leadership when it comes to choosing where and with whom to work. This same leader indicated that communication could and should be worked on from both sides so that a more trusting relationship is established. An Eastern European leader also related, "There must be a certain flexibility . . . from place to place," allowing the indigenous leadership to make those calls when things in the strategy need to be adjusted. In response, Mike Jorgensen, Director of e3 International Strategies, said, "We concur; however, many times we hear 'it won't work that way here,' when we go to an area for the first time. But after the national hosts try it (e3 Partners' model for CP), they find that it does (work)."[99] So we do try to provide that flexibility when it comes to strategy development, and we sometimes ask our national partners to do the same. As a result, we are learning together.

The Need for Extended Training Opportunities

The most frequent response on this item was related to providing more in-depth extended training for the national leaders (both lay and clergy) who will continue the work at the CP site. The weakest link in the model seems to be that nationals, although trained in First Steps CP curriculum during the LDC, are not equipped well enough to disciple all of the new believers following the campaign. This weakness has long been recognized among e3 Partners' Executive Leadership Team and has more recently been addressed in several ways.

Dr. Jerry Wofford, retired professor from the University of Texas at Arlington, is currently splitting time between Dallas Theological Seminary (DTS) and e3 Partners. Dr. Wofford has brought academic expertise to the table and has helped e3 Partners pilot several "Schools for Church Planters" that provide extended training using the Omega Course as its primary curriculum.[100] Several schools have been started in Latin America and East Africa. The goal is to establish at least one of these schools in each of the countries where e3 Partners has on-going work.

In addition to this in-house effort, e3 Partners also has a relationship with several organizations through networking, sometimes referring national leaders for study-at-home opportunities. One of the most in-depth training programs we recommend is the Bible Training Center for Pastors (BTCP), which includes most of the core curriculum of a seminary degree. This material was designed by a DTS graduate and is not necessarily geared toward CP.

One other option that e3 provides national leaders is a CD full of resources called "e3 Church Planting Kit." This is a self-study through many compiled resources with no accountability or reporting back to e3 Partners.

Engaging in Interdependent Partnerships

An unstated but understood goal at e3 Partners is that our ministry be conducive to interdependent partnerships. We have defined that as "a relationship estab-

lished on the basis of common goals and objectives that
are mutually beneficial for all parties involved." The common goal central to all e3 Partners does is establishing
new churches. We do that through mobilizing and equipping both North Americans and nationals for the purpose
of evangelizing the lost and starting reproducing churches. With that in mind, we asked our national leaders
whether or not e3 Partners effectively facilitates interdependent partnerships. There was a unanimous affirma-
tion that we indeed do. One Eastern European leader
stated that he sees e3 Partners as an "intercessor" that
helps churches in North America and in his country to
connect and establish transformational relationships that
result in people coming to faith and churches being established. He went further saying, "e3 is the organization
that motivates people, many of them usually not too
active in their churches, to go and serve the Lord. This
'going' is transforming them and helping these Christians
grow spiritually . . . e3 apparently has nothing to gain,
but without e3 many people would lose greatly."

One Latin American leader adds, "Interdependency
not only involves mutual benefit, but also each party contributes and has responsibilities . . . it implies being
equal." There are indeed responsibilities on all sides.
The sending agency (in this case e3 Partners) is responsible for equipping and providing resources for both STM
teams and national leaders. The national hosts are
responsible for selecting where and with whom we work

and also for the follow-up and on-going supervision of the newly established churches. The goer-guests (STMers) are responsible for being as prepared as possible to go and serve their national brothers and sisters to help them achieve their own indigenous CP goals.

Is e3 Partners Accomplishing its Purpose?

As a core value and stated objective, e3 Partners exists to "help more nationals plant more churches." How are we doing on our central purpose? The nationals, when asked if we are effective at helping to establish churches in their countries, responded with a resounding and unanimous, "Yes!"

One national director from East Africa recounted how a church was first planted in a city two years ago during an e3 campaign that utilized an STM team. To date that church has planted ten others in that city. Another African national director testified that many of the churches have planted second and third generation churches already. How is such rapid reproduction possible? Yet another African leader said, "This model has proven effective in establishing new churches because it does not focus on buildings or other unnecessary things which do not help or assist in evangelism and CP. The model focuses on people, not structures. The tools are also easy to learn and use."

So what about other areas where e3 Partners works? Leaders from the other regions pointed out that the effectiveness of the model to establish churches hinges on the follow-up discipleship of new believers in the area where the church is being started. One leader noted that the national host pastor must really understand the vision for CP before the campaign if the model is going to work. Although retention rates have only just begun to be studied among e3 Partners' church plants, one South American national director has documented that at least 70% of churches started over the last three years are still meeting with most of them growing.[101]

The Perceived Personal Impact of Partnership

One question was related to how national leaders' relationship with e3 Partners has either positively or negatively impacted their ministry. The responses were overwhelmingly positive with almost every leader mentioning how e3 Partners had given them the vision and tools for CP and motivation to actually establish reproducing churches. Several respondents also mentioned how the partnership helped them develop a network of influence within their own countries. One from Eastern Europe stated, "We needed a strategy to start churches in the villages where there are not any believers. When I met the STM teams I understood that the teams were to be a motivation to choose a new church start location and to make contacts preparing the way to spread the Gospel and start new indigenous churches."

A Latin American leader added, "We have been able to use their (e3 Partners') tools to carry out other campaigns without the accompaniment of US teams." In all,

three fourths of the interviewed national leaders emphasized that e3 Partners has positively impacted their ministry by giving them a vision for CP and equipping them
with a reproducible model that nationals can use with or
without North American STM teams.

A Skeptic Turned Believer

One East African man was skeptical of e3 Partners at
first and conducted a thorough investigation by acquiring
the tools and training materials to test them with his own
congregation. After demonstrating how to use the
Evangecube and the e3 Tract, he took a group of lay leaders to a new area and recorded 114 professions of faith
(POFs) and a new church plant in only five days.

Seeing the effectiveness of these new tools and how
their use was not dependent upon the presence of foreign-
ers, the leader decided to try working with an official e3
Partners' campaign inviting a North American STM team
to partner with his church. Interestingly, the results of
that campaign netted almost the same number of POFs
(104) and another new church. Later, that individual was
named our National Director in his country and has over-
seen dozens of STM campaigns both with North
Americans and without. The original church that was
started on his first campaign with e3 Partners in 2000
has reproduced three times in just six years.

Emerging National Strategies

How reproducible is the e3 Partners' model? Earlier I
mentioned research using a control group made up of 42
Peruvian nationals who had taken the e3 Partners' model
and made it their own. The result of this indigenization
of the model is seen in the fact that one Peruvian leader
has 7 campaigns with North Americans planned for 2007,
while during the same period he is directing dozens of
national-only campaigns! Some of these may even be
sent to neighboring countries in South America. That
same national leader is the pastor of a house church in
Lima, Peru that has planted 14 daughter churches, each
led by one of his disciples. In addition, his house church
has sent 4 full-time missionaries to South Asia and
another 2 are preparing to go. Granted, e3 Partners can
in no way take credit for all that God has done through
any of its national leaders, but most nationals would be
quick to tell you they caught the vision and learned the
basics initially while participating with an e3 STM team.

This type of indigenization of the e3 model is not limited to the country of Peru. We see similar ownership
among nationals on every continent in which we are
working. In Ethiopia, God is using e3 Partners to help a
denomination in its goal to double its 6000 churches in a
matter of just a few years. In Romania, the national leaders have taken the momentum gained through participation with e3 Partners and are now planting churches

throughout their country and even among the diasporas of Romanians all over Europe. In India one national leader has taken much of what he learned in working with e3 Partners and has adapted it to train a small army of national church planters through several schools he has established.

Beyond Expectations

When the kindling of equipped national leaders is arranged and the match of a North American STM team is struck strategically, fires emerge and spread. e3 Partners is only a small part of the equation that brings about these wildfires. It is God's mission, and it is facilitated most effectively through indigenous leadership. We at e3 Partners have simply attempted to encourage the real professional pyros through interdependent partnerships and catalytic events we call church planting campaigns. I believe the research presented in this chapter proves we have succeeded in so doing beyond our own expectations.

Part 3
A Match Made in Heaven

The Development and Evaluation of the e3 Partners' Model for Church Planting using Strategic Short-term Missions.

In order for STM to be strategic, it must be tied into a long-term strategy with its primary purpose being to help its national hosts to reach their own people and beyond through reproductive church planting. This is the approach taken by e3 Partners, which is an STM organization built upon a long-term, national-driven strategy. The ministry of e3 Partners has developed on the leading edge of several recent paradigm shifts in missions. The rapid onset of globalization in the wake of WWII, along with Western cultural shifts, have contributed to the desire among churches and laity to become more active participants in the completion of the Great Commission. As a result, many STM organizations, including e3 Partners have emerged to help facilitate the movement. In addition to this, the methodological focus of missions in the latter part of the 20th century shifted toward the concept of indigenous CPMs. e3 Partners has sought to combine the catalytic manpower of STM with the focus of CP in order to result in a strategic approach to cross-cultural missions. We believe that this combination is a match made in heaven.

Chapter 10

Serendipity

*Serendipity is finding something unexpected and useful
while searching for something else entirely.*[102]

Historical Roots of e3 Partners

Any adequate understanding of e3 Partners requires
going back to its origins as Global Missions Fellowship
(GMF), and even further to the cultural context within
which the organization arose.[103]   As mentioned earlier,
the phenomenon of STM as we know it today began to
emerge in the 1960s as several cultural shifts were taking
place in the West. Globalization sprung forth as the perception of the world became smaller and what has been
dubbed as the Boomer generation (those born around the

end of WWII) began to shape American culture. Whereas
Evangelical Christians from the Builder generation before
them had been satisfied with supporting missions
through finances, this new generation wanted to person-
alize the Great Commission by becoming directly
involved. It was in this era that within the ranks of
Southern Baptists (SBC) something called "Partnership
Missions" arose. Although there was some initial resist-
ance within the then Foreign Mission Board (now
International Mission Board of the SBC), the concept of
using short-term volunteers has become a major factor
along with its career field missionaries.

e3 Parteners President, Curtis Hail notes, "This movement really began to take substantial form and might be
said to have officially begun in 1970 as Robert Gunn, who
now serves on the Board of Directors for e3 Partners, and
other laymen traveled with Dub Jackson of the FMB to
(work as STMers in) Japan." According to Hail, Jackson
was committed to the idea of forming direct partnerships
between SBC churches in the U.S. and churches emerging overseas." Jackson later took his idea and his experience in his retirement years and developed the concept of
Partnership Missions. From this sprang the World
Evangelism Fellowship (WEF) which was started by a
group of SBC laymen who had experienced what God
could do through STM ventures and wanted to share that
with others. Jackson continued to refine the methodology
of WEF while working in Asia, but another leader

emerged named Ben Meith who formed International Crusades, an organization that brought STM to the more nearby country of Mexico.

It was not until 1980 that an SBC pastor from Oklahoma named Mike Downey participated in one of WEF's partnership projects in South Korea. While on that journey, Downey realized the potential for mobilizing the laity to witness using simple tools in the power of the Holy Spirit. Hail notes that Downey's philosophy of ministry was shaped by his experience with WEF, particularly the empowerment of the laity joining in the Great Commission. As Senior Pastor of FBC Hennessey, Oklahoma, Downey sought to lead his church toward being more involved in missions. One of the first steps was to invite Ramon Aleman, a Cuban-born evangelist and church planter, to be the pastor of a Hispanic mission within his church. Downey had previously served as a teacher in a mission school in Mexico prior to attending Dallas Theological Seminary (DTS), and thus he had gained a heart for reaching Latin Americans.

We Found What We Weren't Looking For

In 1984, Downey and Aleman put together a group of laymen from their church and partnered with a national church in Chihuahua, Mexico in an evangelistic outreach using some of the methods picked up on that earlier WEF trip to South Korea. The group saw many people make professions of faith in Christ during the STM journey;

however, they did not realize how successful the week had been until they discovered what the national pastor did upon their departure. Overwhelmed with the number of new believers in one particular barrio, the Mexican pastor decided the only way to ensure that these people would be adequately discipled and ministered to was to start a new church among them. Thus, without prior planning, Downey, Aleman and the national pastor stumbled onto what has become a distinctive of e3 Partners – mobilizing STM teams to partner with national churches in an evangelistic outreach that results in new churches being planted. Hail likens this serendipitous discovery to what Peter Drucker calls "The Unexpected Success."[104] He quips that Downey pondered, "That worked awfully well accidentally! I wonder if we could start a church on purpose?" From that point forward Downey and Aleman sought out such partnership opportunities all over Mexico and then mobilized STM teams from the U.S. to engage in this newfound method of cross-cultural church planting.[105] Over the next several years these campaigns were held in Monterrey, Mexico City, Cuernavaca, and Guadalajara, each birthing multiple new congregations as national mother churches targeted unreached neighborhoods.

The Vision Emerges

It was not long before the Mexico Baptist Convention heard about the movement that was underway, and they called its accidental leaders in for consultation to see how

they could capitalize on the phenomenon. Following
those meetings, the Convention adopted the strategy as
their official CP methodology asking Downey to work
with them from the U.S.. Word travels fast in ministry
circles, and it was not long before one of the most respect-
ed SBC pastors in the U.S., Dr. W.A. Criswell of FBC
Dallas, invited Downey to come and serve in an unpaid
role designated as "Minister of Church Planting." The
influence of Dr. Criswell garnered for Downey a vast network of churches that were interested in engaging in
strategic STM. There, in 1987, Downey organized and
officially incorporated "Global Missions Fellowship"
(GMF).

In the mid-1980s Hail had his own first STM experience in Malawi, Africa. On that initial STM journey, Hail
and the team from Richardson Heights Baptist Church
saw over three thousand people make professions of faith.
The magnitude of Malawian responsiveness haunted Hail
as he returned to the U.S. wondering what would happen
to those new babes in Christ. After a conversation with
Downey, the idea of intentional CP using evangelistic
STM teams partnered with national churches became the
answer to the question of how to conserve the harvest.
Hail decided to join Downey on a trip to Mexico City to see
this strategy up close, and at the end of that campaign over
fifty new "mission churches" had been started.[106] He
recounts that, "It was the 'dual impact' nature of the ministry that was so very exciting. In addition to the salva-

tions and the new churches 'over there,' it is also the changed lives and renewed churches 'over here' . . . ." Following that campaign, Hail, then a student at DTS, decided to pursue an opportunity to be a LTM with OC International in Europe. After several roadblocks prevented him from moving overseas, Downey called again, this time asking Hail to join him as one of the first full-time staff members of GMF. Downey recognized the cultural shift taking place and its effect on the missions movement, and the two capitalized because "this (rise of STM) was something many traditional mission agencies were neither expecting nor equipped to cope with in those early days." Hail traces his and Downey's involvement in the STM movement less to their own ingenuity or planning than to their spiritual DNA as emerging Baby-Boomer leaders. He summarizes,

> *GMF caught a movement that God was already whipping into full force – the movement of lay participation directly on the foreign mission field. A movement that said to the nationals, 'Rather than come permanently to do your work for you, let us come alongside you for a time to help and encourage you – to model (strategic) ministry for you and to bring resources for you to fulfill YOUR (sic.) role in the Great Commission.*

GMF Riding the Wave of a Movement

The 1990s brought many new opportunities for GMF along with an expanding staff to be able to seize them. The growth forced Downey and Hail to clarify GMF's

vision from the seminal state of running more and more
campaigns each year to the more measurable and yet still
simplistic: "Mobilize the Body of Christ to help put a local
church in every neighborhood of the world." (Or variously
stated as, "Mobilize the Body of Christ to help put a local
church within walking distance of every person on
earth.") The original plan was, as the staff grew, to
expand CP campaigns southward through all of Latin
America. Hail jokes that in those early days, "We
planned to get to Tierra Del Fuego and then look around
and decide where to go next!" Little did they know how
quickly they would face some of those strategic decisions
as world events would open doors previously closed to
Western missionaries.

"Beginning in 1989 and through 1990," Hail recounts,
"God brought about cataclysmic changes in the geo-political world . . . as the Iron Curtain fell and the East opened
up to GMF and the North American Church." By 1991
Downey and Hail decided to capitalize on the newfound
freedoms of the former Soviet Union and through several
contacts mobilized STM teams to penetrate Russia,
Ukraine and Romania. By expanding the ministry of
GMF to Eastern Europe, an ever-growing throng of U.S.
churches were attracted to the opportunities to engage in
partnership-style missions.

Out of this increase of mobilized churches came a flow
of new GMF staff members. One of the first to join GMF
was the current VP for International Ministries, attorney

Mike Jorgensen. Another key leader to join in those early years was New Jersey pastor, Sam Ingrassia. Ingrassia, who continues today as an e3 Partners Executive Team member, had experience mobilizing his own church for STM ventures in Haiti. Like so many others that eventually joined GMF, he was interested in the CP distinctive he felt made the ministry strategic. Within a few years GMF attracted Dan Hitzhusen, a former Campus Crusade for Christ and Josh McDowell Ministries staffer. Hitzhusen's experience traveling into many restricted access countries helped to expand the horizon for GMF even more, taking the organization into what has become known as the "10/40 Window." Hitzhusen still serves with e3, now as the Director of e3 Mission, coordinating all of our STM campaigns. He is also responsible for starting our West Regional Office in San Diego, CA. Dozens of individuals caught that early vision and joined GMF to ride the wave of the STM movement, some of whom are still on staff and some who have moved on to other opportunities. Hail summarizes the history of growth at GMF in the following way:

> *The story of GMF from the late 80s through the late 90s is one of a pioneering group who really sacrificed to lay a foundation for the ministry . . . .Many came and went, used by God for a season, and a steadfast few persevered, determined by God's grace to see the vision become a reality . . . It is a story full of judgment errors and human foibles, none intentional . . .*

(and) a greater story of God's love and patience, His grace and sufficiency to accomplish His purposes in spite of, not because of His servants! It is a story of God's grace taking this unlikely three to a staff of over 200 fulltime and associates to date; from working in one country to over fifty; from an annual budget of $155,000 in 1990 to over $12 million in 2005.[108]

Amazingly through the massive growth at GMF in the 1990s, the organization has maintained the original vision for using STM teams to catalyze national CP efforts. As with any growing organization, a move away from the original vision is inevitable when new staff is added unless there are safeguards against such a drift.

Refining the Vision and Shifting the Focus

In 1998 at the behest of Dan Hitzhusen, the GMF Executive Team gathered for its first strategic planning meeting. With the help of several outside consultants, the leadership team came to realize that they were falling far short of the vague goals they had previously made public. At that point they realized that running more and more campaigns could never achieve the goal of helping the Church in fulfilling the Great Commission. In order to achieve organizational objectives, GMF had to shift the focus from merely increasing STM mobilization to a more strategic CP equipping and empowering force for national leaders. Hail recounts, "We began to see the U.S. mobilization of lay STM teams not so much as the fires of national CP initiatives, but as the matches for such fires . . . and this was a major shift for us."[104]

In the wake of this organizational paradigm shift, the leadership team at GMF adopted a strategic plan that, "called for defining key concepts, identifying key partners, and developing key tools and materials." After these objectives were met, GMF began to "export those strategic resources to our national partners to empower them to plant countless more churches on their own . . . shifting the focus of our ministry from 'us' to 'them'."[109]

Simplicity as a Core Value

One of the hallmarks of GMF up to this point was that it took something that seemed so complex, namely church planting, and made it simple enough that lay leaders could participate. Because none of GMF's founders were missiologists by training, they intentionally looked for ways to keep things simple so lay leaders would engage in the Great Commission.

In 1998, God brought another serendipitous idea GMF's way. Staff member Craig Poston had just returned from leading a trip to Haiti where he had used storyboards to share the Gospel with the illiterate there. Another new staffer named Nathan Sheets (now the Director of Development for e3 Partners) with a marketing background took an unfolding novelty advertising cube and remarked, "Wouldn't it be great if we could put the Gospel on a cube like this?" A third staff member,

Jim Wyatt, came back the next day with that cube and a bunch of sketches made on Post-It notes unfolding to share the core components of the Gospel. This idea was refined and then produced by Sheets' elder brother Jeff and within a year Evangecubes hit the market throughout the U.S. as a tool that makes sharing the Gospel simple enough for anyone.[110]

The GMF staff implemented this new resource into its CP campaigns by equipping STMers and nationals alike to use the Cube as a tool for helping lead people to faith in Christ. The success of the Evangecube soon forced the leadership team to create a sister organization, and Curtis Hail threw his experience into that ring to help the Sheets brothers get it off the ground. All the while GMF and Evangecube Ministries struggled to figure out how they could not just co-exist, but actually become catalysts for one another.

Three Ministries under One Umbrella

As the Millennium turned, yet another event rocked the geo-political landscape and forced missions agencies to make adjustments to a world where terrorism would soon become the norm. The tragic events of the terrorist attacks on September 11th, 2001 only reinforced among the leadership team at GMF that the ministry needed to focus even more on other ways to facilitate CP besides just the mobilization of STM teams from North America. As a result, the leadership team went back to the counsel

they received at their earlier 1998 strategic planning
meeting that entailed several suggestions:

1. Remain focused on the mission to stimulate CP.
2. Diversify methods and strategies while
   remaining true to the mission of CP.
3. Look for ways to involve more donors and
   strategic partners.
4. Increase synergy among the existing
   ministries (GMF & Evangecube).

Downey, the instrument God had used to birth the
GMF vision over fifteen years earlier, left to pursue other
ministry opportunities. But his influence and original
vision for getting laity involved in evangelistic outreaches
through the establishment of new churches has remained
intact to this day. Downey's departure forced the ministry to unify around its purpose and resulted ultimately
in reorganization under a new umbrella called Global
Partners headed by Curtis Hail. Hail's job during those
days of transition was not one to be envied. Under his
watch, however, the leadership structures of GMF and
Evangecube were brought back together along with
another sister ministry called GoLeaders.net (GLN). This
latter organization had been birthed out of GMF in order
to focus on developing leaders for CP. GLN was started
in an attempt to train an army of national church
planters.[111] By reorganizing under the name Global
Partners, the strengths of each of the ministries was har-
nessed to achieve the objectives set forth at the 1998
strategic planning meeting.

From GMF to e3 Partners

Although this reorganization started in 2002, it really was not completed until early 2005 when the renewed synergy and CP focus culminated in the re-branding of the entire ministry as one unified organization called e3 Partners. This name was chosen after boiling down the identity and purpose behind all that we do into three words: equip, evangelize and establish. Finally, what had started as a serendipitous discovery in Mexico and spread to a global CP organization, became refined and polished to the point where its God-centered mission statement is both measurable and memorable: "e3 Partners exists to equip God's people to evangelize the lost and establish new churches."

According to Hail, "(e3 Partners') mission was always fixed, but our understanding of our role in accomplishing that mission became more sophisticated . . . and our methods became a bit more flexible in order to adapt to changing circumstances in the world." In considering ways in which to diversify methods at e3 Partners, the leadership team decided that several factors must be considered. First, the method must help us maintain relevance to the trans-cultural churches we serve. Second, the method must increase the results of what we do; namely, helping more nationals plant more churches.

The reorganization and re-branding provided the perfect opportunity to begin to diversify our methods to reflect the paradigm shift toward a national-centered CP ministry that continues to utilize, but is not limited solely to the presence of North American STM teams. Hail recalls a discussion from the 1998 strategic planning meeting where they spoke of, "our national partners taking the model and tools we empowered them with in our campaigns and then they would carry on replicating the model over for themselves on a much larger scale."[112]   Not long after that conversation David Garrison's book on CPMs was released. The principles set forth embodied and to a degree described what was happening in many locations where GMF was working.[113]   Hail continues:

> *We found ourselves, purely by the grace of God, right at the forefront of missions thinking and on the front of the wave that would sweep and captivate the entire world missions enterprise. Today, most ministries have shifted to church planting and focusing on igniting indigenous movements.*[114]

Even with the reorganization toward a more national-centered strategy, STM mobilization remains important to e3 Partners. Hail explains that these teams serve the role of "incarnate vision casting" by modeling and encouraging the nationals in their CP initiatives. Hail goes on to say that,

> *While theoretically we are open to any new strategy that plants more churches even if it requires us to lay aside the mobilization of STM teams, in truth we feel strongly that in part God has raised up e3 Partners and our vehicle, e3 Mission Teams, to play a distinct, if not unique role in the CP arena.*[115]

The idea is that STM can be strategic when it is a part of a long-term indigenous CP strategy. While some STM agencies make the transformation of the goer-guest the primary impetus, e3 Partners believes such transformation is more lasting when the purpose of the journey is well-defined and national-centered.[116]

One of the new ways e3 Partners has sought to achieve the objective of helping more nationals plant more churches is through the "e3 Partnership Program." In this program, e3 Partners seek out promising national leaders with a passion and vision for starting indigenous CPMs in their countries and beyond. These leaders help coordinate e3 STM campaigns that involve North Americans and replicate that model to coordinate national-only campaigns.[117] Because this requires a good bit of travel and full-time attention, e3 Partners created a sustained-giving program where these appointed National Directors (ND) receive a modest salary, CP resources and an operating budget. This enables the ND to recruit and equip an army of nationals – lay and clergy alike – to be trained in e3's *First Steps: Mobilizing Your Church into God's Harvest Fields*, CP curriculum to share the Gospel using the Evangecube, and then to mobilize teams of nationals to target neighborhoods to establish new churches. Sam Ingrassia metaphorically comments on the effectiveness of this new addition to e3's methodology:

> *"Give a man a fish. What have you done? You feed him for a day. Teach a man to fish. What have you*

done? Conventional wisdom says 'You feed him for a lifetime.' NO! You have only given him the hope to feed himself for a lifetime. But if you show him how to fish, then you give him the rod and tackle . . . you have helped to feed him and his community for a lifetime."[118]

e3 Partners shows leaders how to mobilize and establish new churches via the use of STM teams and then provides them with the tools and materials to equip God's people to evangelize their communities and establish small groups and churches. In doing so, Hail says, "We have equipped and empowered the nationals for CPMs."[119] As of 2006, there were national directors appointed in over a dozen countries working under this methodology. In the future where e3 Partners works will be evaluated based upon whether or not we have a national leader in place to facilitate these catalytic movements.

A recent marketing campaign at e3 Partners goes back to that seminal mission statement and personalizes it by stating, "If Sarah can't walk to church, she can't go to church. So help take the church to her."[120] The point of these advertisements is to get North American Christians to partner with our national directors by praying, giving, and going to be a part of establishing reproducing churches that will hopefully reach every neighborhood in the world.

Thus, while the ministry of GMF started by being built upon the North American STM teams, the ministry of e3 Partners simply leverages North American STM teams and partners as another tool or resource to supplement otherwise indigenous CPMs. This paradigm shift away from emphasizing the experience of the goer-guest and toward emphasizing the church planting vision of our national host is what sets e3 Partners use of STM teams apart and makes it truly strategic.

Striking the Match

Chapter 11

How's it Goin'?

"The fire and wood are here" **Genesis 22:7**

Organizational Goals

e3 Partners is church planting ministry that utilizes STM teams as a core component of its strategy. The non-negotiable is intentional CP, not STM. Missiologist David Hesselgrave has said,

> *"The primary mission of the Church, and therefore of churches, is to proclaim the Gospel of Christ and gather believers into local churches where they can be built up in the faith and made effective in service, thereby planting new congregations throughout the world."*[121]

So how is e3 Partners doing at CP? What strengths and weaknesses have emerged within the organization's model for CP? Following the reorganization from GMF to e3 Partners mentioned in chapter ten, it became clear that prior goals were nebulous and immeasurable. So under the new mission statement (Equip, Evangelize and Establish) the leadership team set forth new organizational goals that allowed progress to be tracked. The stated "faith goals" of e3 Partners as of 2006 are to:

1. Equip ten million Christians to
2. Evangelize one billion people and
3. Establish one million new churches.

Evaluation must be in relation to how far the ministry has come toward reaching these numeric goals.

Evaluation

Since becoming e3 Partners, how is the organization doing in working toward these goals? This chapter shows that e3 Partners is indeed making progress. Each graph contains information reported at various points throughout the history of the organization. Keep in mind that there was a significant transitional period as e3 Partners emerged from GMF. The year 2000 was just prior to the reorganization. The year 2003 was during the middle of the reorganization. And the years 2005-2006 were immediately following the reorganization from GMF to e3 Partners. This latter period marks the paradigm shift in the organization where the pendulum of emphasis completed the swing from "How many STM teams can we mobilize?" to "How can we help more nationals plant more churches?" There was a significant increase in professions of faith, churches planted and nationals trained following the reorganization. As would be expected, the figures during the midst of the transition show a slight decline or stagnation in some areas. This might possibly be due to intra-organizational issues in trying to get the nearly 200 staff on board with the change. The overall effect of the transition netted overwhelmingly positive results.

Equip

The stated goal of equipping more nationals is indirectly tied to the mobilization of North American STM teams in that, each time a team goes out, they partner with more nationals and help provide much needed momentum to begin the CP process. Granted, most of these STM teams are hardly expert missionaries. They have, however, been trained in how to share their testimony, a simple Gospel message, disciple a small group of new believers, gather them for small group worship, and develop the national leaders with whom they are partnering. Therefore, mobilization of STM teams contributes significantly to the equipping goals of e3 Partners.

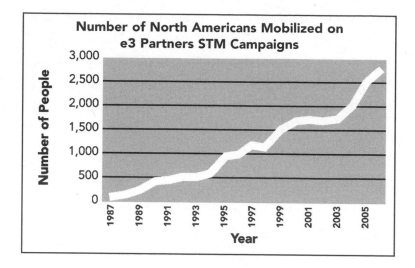

When looking at the graph above, it is evident that there has been a steady increase in the number of North Americans mobilized throughout e3's twenty-year history. When these STM teams are adequately oriented beforehand, the potential for equipping nationals for CP is maximized.

It is even easier to get a grasp of the paradigm shift that took place in the emergence of e3 Partners by looking at the following graph where the number of nationals mobilized/equipped is divided by various periods in the history of the ministry's development. The first period ranged from the inception of GMF in 1987 up to 1996 where the ministry focused more on mobilizing more STM teams and less on national strategies. The number of nationals mobilized and equipped for CP in that period was just over 14,000.

In 1997 the organization began to change, at which point it held its first strategy planning conference and clarified both purpose and goals. On the heels of that event transition occurred which first resulted in a temporary structure called Global Partners, and then the formulation for a comprehensive ministry that would bring together several branches of the ministry that had been operating with different and sometimes conflicting goals. This second period in the ministry resulted in just over 50,000 nationals mobilized and equipped for CP.

By the year 2005, the ministry had completely reorganized around many of the suggestions formulated in that prior strategy planning consultation, and the result was the birth of e3 Partners, which exists to equip God's people to evangelize the lost and establish new churches. The latter two tenets of that statement have been largely supported by the growth in the first, for in 2005-2006 alone e3 was able to equip and mobilize just over 200,000 nationals for involvement in CP work! The ministry is well on its way to its stated goal of ten million, and with an exponentially growing network of national trainers, it may not be far off. In fact, the number of national leaders attending a First Steps LDC has risen from under 2,500 in the year 2000 to over 6200 in 2006.[122] These figures only include LDCs conducted by North Americans. Through the new e3 Partnership strategy, our NDs are equipping many more - 167,086 in 2006 alone.[123]

Evangelize

When God brought the concept for the Evangecube to the ministry of GMF back in the late 1990s, no one ever dreamed that it would become such a globally recognized and utilized tool for sharing the Gospel. It was during that same period of time that the concept of "storying" the Gospel started to be discussed among missions organizations as a result of an increased awareness of literacy issues. When those first Cubes were taken out and test-driven on GMF campaigns, it was quickly recognized that the tool aided in the often challenging job of cross-cultural communication of the Gospel. In fact, by looking closely at graph on the opposite page, it is plain that the number of professions of faith (POF) rose sharply following 1999 – the year the Evangecube was introduced and piloted on GMF campaigns. Since that time there has been a steady increase in POFs reported on campaigns involving North American STM teams. The twenty-year total for POFs reported on these STM campaigns is 641,560.[124]

The tremendous number of reported POFs on STM campaigns is quite an amazing testimony to God's hand on the ministry. However, the paradigm shift toward e3 Partners has yielded even more astonishing reports. The following graph displays how in the three years since the transition towards emphasis on equipping more nationals for CP, the number of POFs reported by those nationals is over half the twenty-year total for campaigns that

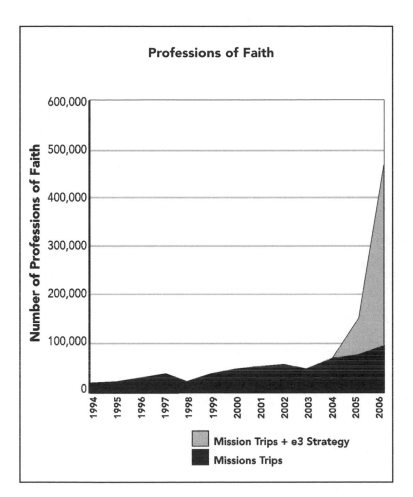

involved STM teams. In fact, a quick glance at the graph
on page 158 shows that in both 2005 and 2006 the nationals equipped by e3 Partners have led over three times as
many people to faith in Jesus Christ. The amazing thing
about this is that virtually every one of those nationals
has been empowered and challenged to reproduce themselves by training someone else.

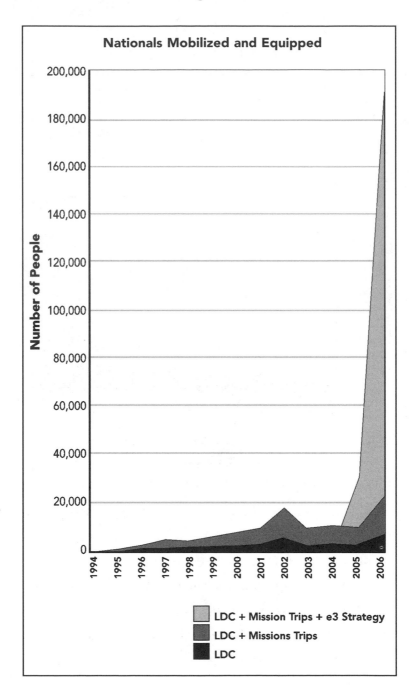

Nationals Mobilized and Equipped

Thus far all that I have displayed are the numbers of those who have been evangelized and went on to make a public profession of faith in Jesus. The stated goal of evangelizing one billion people takes into account that not all of those evangelized will make a profession of faith. The next graph displays how the number of people reported as "evangelized" experienced a sharp, exponential increase at the end of the transition to e3 Partners. Keep in mind that these are only those Gospel presentations that are recorded. Countless numbers go unrecorded for various reasons on STM and national-only campaigns alike.[125] By the end of 2006 the ministry had recorded a cumulative total of 3,233,663 persons evangelized – virtually all of which occurred in either a small group or personal Gospel presentation.

The trend lines displayed here are bound to continue as more and more nationals are equipped and mobilized to evangelize the lost with simple tools like the Evangecube and simple training like First Steps. The stated goal of evangelizing one billion people, roughly one-sixth of the world's population, still seems distant. But left in the hands of the trained professionals alone, that task would be impossible.[126] By equipping an army of lay leaders with simple tools and a simple strategy, both of which are trans-cultural, e3 Partners is bound to make a significant contribution to the task of world evangelization with its grassroots emphasis.

Establish

If the key to making STM strategic is tying it in to the longer-term strategy of CP, then e3 Partners is at least moving in the right direction. By this I mean that the organization has kept CP as its distinctive since its inception under Downey's leadership back in the 1980s. It would have been very easy to get sidetracked and go down other roads in order to mobilize more North Americans. Construction trips, VBS and prayer-walking opportunities abound in the realm of STM partially because they are not as spiritually demanding as evangelism and CP. I praise God that the leadership has kept this purpose at the forefront. Since the transition to e3 Partners, the CP emphasis seems to only be increasing.

The following graph displays the number of churches planted on STM campaigns over the twenty-year history of the organization. That serendipitous beginning in Mexico has grown into an intentional and productive CP force. With ten of the organization's twenty years yielding more than 300 CPs annually, one wonders why anyone is still skeptical. I can think of dozens of first-hand examples of 2nd or 3rd generation churches that have replicated to become catalysts in what some might consider CPMs. It should be noted that as the focus has shifted toward a more national-centered strategy, the STM campaigns have only improved in their own results with the last two years both topping 500 Church Planted. In its twenty-year history the organization has partnered

national churches and leaders together with North
American STM teams to help birth over 5,500 new
churches in nearly 50 different countries around the
world. But in the last two years alone, national-only campaigns with no North American STM teams have reported 4,700 new church starts! Based upon these facts it can
not be disputed that e3 Partners does indeed help more
nationals plant more churches – keeping true to its mission statement. Though the goal of one million churches
is still a long way off, the key is not just starting new
churches, but establishing reproducing churches.

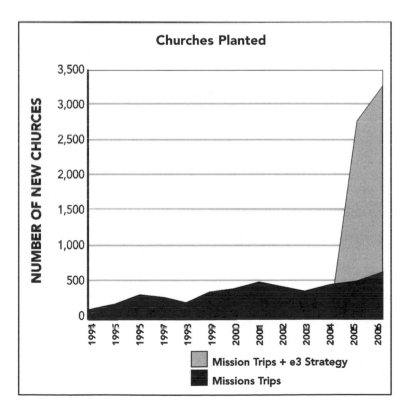

Churches Planted

As I have previously mentioned, e3 Partners has not kept records on most of the church plants that they have participated in over the years because the organization has never considered itself as a supervisor to mother churches, much less a denomination. Instead, e3 has focused on forging interdependent partnerships with national leaders and churches to help them plant reproducing churches through equipping them, helping them evangelize the lost around them, and casting vision and providing momentum towards the end of establishing healthy churches. And healthy churches reproduce. Whether or not the churches that e3 Partners has helped to plant are surviving, much less reproducing, is a matter that has only briefly been looked into.[127] However, plans are already underway to track the growth and health of churches that are currently being planted. If that future research proves to be favorable for e3 Partners, then both missiologists and LTM personnel will be forced to take notice that STM can be used in a strategic manner. And if that occurs, we are likely to see the missiological paradigm shift toward direct involvement swing with even more force in the years to come.

Fire!

How's it goin' at e3 Partners? By the looks at the reports found in this chapter things are going well and getting better all the time. Sparks flew over twenty years ago on a single serendipitous journey to Mexico. Since that time matches have been struck through STM church planting campaigns in nearly fifty countries around the globe. Over the course of the ministry's history many lessons have been learned from our national partners helping us to become more and more strategic in our approach to equip, evangelize and establish. We have learned how to arrange the kindling in a way that fewer matches are being wasted these days. And the most exciting thing of all is that indigenous national leaders are now striking matches of their own by reproducing the strategy, sometimes with no North American STM teams at all. A few of those flames are spreading beyond what can be managed with human ingenuity. Nationals are being encouraged and equipped. Lives are changing as an army of leaders, both lay and clergy, are reorienting their lives around the Great Commission. Churches are being established intentionally and with a vision for rapid reproduction. At e3 Partners we are not playing with matches . . . we're using them strategically to start wildfires.

Striking the Match

Chapter 12
Keep the Fire Burning

"Do not put out the Spirit's fire" **1 Thessalonians 5:19**

Don't Douse the Flame

Many professionals in the realm of missions have launched complaints against the rising tide of what comes under the banner of STM. One of the most common is that STM teams are often culturally insensitive. I agree that when STM goes bad, it has the potential to go really bad. However, I wonder if the mistakes made by the average STMer are not magnified in some respects because we are easy targets. What about the mistakes so often made by traditional missionaries in the past? In the 19th century missionaries were often unintentional agents of imperialism. In the early 20th century well-meaning paternalism held indigenous leaders in a death grip squelching the rise of anything that looked as if it would go beyond the administrative control of Western missionaries. Just a few decades ago traditional field-based missionaries were busy building churches, hospitals, and orphanages with funds and blueprints from the West. Most have made an about-face and now discourage such practices. I wonder what the next generation of missiologists will say of those who are currently on the field. I'm sure there will be lessons learned from our generation as well; some good and some not so good. Whatever our strategy, it has become painfully evident that indigenous leadership must be at the center and in the driver's seat. What is at stake if we fail to understand that?

Like Water on a Flame

The flames of church planting are burning all over the world. But just because a flame ignites doesn't mean it will become a wildfire. And even if it does, these spiritual movements are much easier to put out than those physical flames that dot the North American landscape each summer. David Garrison notes in his book *Church Planting Movements* that CPMs are susceptible to fading or even failing should the expatriate professional missionary take too central a role. He makes it clear that, "you begin with the torch in their (indigenous national leader's) hand . . .

and the laity is clearly in the driver's seat. Unpaid, non-professional common men and women are leading the churches (in CPMs)."[128] Therefore, Garrison points out that the cross-cultural missionary should play more of a behind the scenes coaching role by meeting with national lay leaders and empowering them to make all the crucial decisions, chief among them training other leaders and planting new churches.

In an admonition to the reader, Garrison included a chapter on the "Seven Deadly Sins" responsible for preventing or halting a CPM. One of the greatest hindrances to the missionary enterprise is the exporting of Western cultural practices that have no grounding in Scripture, yet have been made into sacred cows. Church buildings, formalized training for pastors, paid staff, music styles, requirements for baptism, cultural mores, and clothing styles are just a few so-called "improvements." Yet another danger is the introduction of foreign funds for the wrong purposes. Missionaries have witnessed first hand the adverse consequences of linking money to the advancement of the gospel. Garrison aptly describes it: "Building a movement on foreign funds is like running a machine with an extension cord that stretches across the ocean. When the movement reaches the end of the cord's length, it will abruptly stop."[129] I have witnessed the fall out in Latin America where many churches are not interested in talking about planting new churches unless the funds for a new building follow.

I have worked with pastors that were recipients of such buildings (not by my own design), and they had no inclination of moving beyond the comfortable positions they were cursed with!

An Empowering Approach to Missions

So what can be done to prevent the flickering flames of potential CPMs around the world from being doused with water? Nurturing those flames means we Westerners are going to have to empower indigenous leadership and take a less dominant role. Addressing this issue has been one of the emerging strengths of the e3 Partners' model for church planting using STM teams. Yes, the teams are highly visible, but not for long. These teams do not dictate strategy to the national leadership, but rather go to serve an existing national-led strategy. This places the North American in the periphery of the strategy and the indigenous leadership as central. In many respects, we encourage the national leadership to view our teams as a non-renewable resource to help them reach their church planting goals. When handled properly, the STM teams generate interest in the Gospel message and in the new work emerging in a community. The initial interest is sustained by on-going relationships between nationals long after the STM team is gone. In this way, the STM team is viewed as a match – a resource to help achieve the goal of a wildfire rather than a fireman to control or douse the flames.

The Match was God's Plan All Along

e3 Partners proves that strategic STM can play an important role within the *missio dei*. Jesus said in Matthew 16:18 that He would build His Church, and the Gates of Hades would never prevail against it. We all need to be reminded that where the Church is being established, God is at work. It is my prayer that this book has encouraged you to understand that God can, and often does, use "the least of these" to do extra-ordinary things – all so He can get the glory.

Ultimately this book has not been so much about the e3 Partners' model for church planting or even about strategic STM as about God's mission to redeem a lost world to Himself. In Leviticus 6:13 the priests were warned, "The fire must be kept burning on the altar continuously; it must not go out." As believer priests we all have inherited that exhortation. It was not e3 Partners' idea to equip indigenous leadership and STM teams to evangelize the lost and establish new churches. We believe it was God's plan all along. We're just enjoying being part of a "match made in heaven." It is our hope that this book will help you as a believer priest to take part in God's global plan of redemption as He uses you to ignite and spread wildfires for your joy and His glory.

Striking the Match

Appendix 1
The Acts Strategy Matrix

		Target Area			
		Jerusalem	Judea	Samaria	Ends/Earth
Level of Involvement	Prayer & Advocacy				
	Projects				
	Partnerships				
	Adoption				

Acts Strategy Matrix Terms Defined:

Jerusalem
Any location within the daily sphere of influence of your community of faith.

Judea
Any location outside of the daily sphere of influence of your community of faith, but shares a common worldview.

Samaria
Any location outside of the daily sphere of influence of your community of faith that has a slightly differing worldview, but shares some commonalities.

Ends of the Earth

Any location outside of the daily sphere of influence of your community of faith that has a radically differing worldview with few, if any, commonalities.

Prayer & Advocacy

Any activity of promotion through education, prayer or financial commitment.

Project

Any on-site activity with pre-determined goals that are completed in a single visit.

Partnership

Any on-going activities (both on and off-site) for the achievement of a specified set of goals shared between your community of faith and other Great Commission Christians in the area. Upon completion of shared goals the partnership may be dissolved or re-defined.

Adoption

A life-long commitment to a specific location or people. This commitment involves a relationship that involves, but is not limited to any pre-determined set of goals.

Remember, one of the obstacles to successful church planting is a step-by-step approach. One way that you could implement the Acts Matrix is to identify key leaders within your church that will lead a target group. To do so you would have a "Jerusalem Team", a "Judea Team", a "Samaria Team", and an "Ends of the Earth Team". The responsibility of each team would be to identify ways in which your church is already involved in their target area and move the church toward multiplication in that area. Make sure you do not focus only on your "Jerusalem" – keep in mind what God did to the first church when they made that mistake! Start where you are and move outward and soon you will find a church planting vision permeating your local church Body.

Where are the weaknesses of your church according to the information you put on Matrix?

Where are your strengths?

How will you implement a comprehensive Acts 1:8 approach in your church?

Appendix 2
Summary of Qualitative Research Findings

With regards to the LDC:

- e3 Partners' LDC is crucial to the establishment of CP vision among national pastors and lay leaders.

- e3 Partners' LDC does in fact equip leaders with the simple tools necessary to establish new churches.

With regards to the STM Campaign:

- e3 Partners' STM teams help provide an entrée to the lost in their communities.

- e3 Partners' STM teams provide CP initiative, motivation and momentum.

- e3 Partners' STM teams must be better oriented to the host culture prior to arrival.

General notations:

- e3 Partners provides the vision and tools for CP and the motivation to establish reproducing churches.

- e3 Partners is equipping nationals with a "reproducible model" that can be used with or without North American STM teams.

- e3 Partners empowers nationals to establish indigenous churches.

- e3 Partners effectively facilitates interdependent partnerships.

General recommendations:

- e3 Partners should always extend its focus longer than just a single STM campaign in any given area.

- e3 Partners should consider ways to build more lasting relationships with the churches that they have helped to plant.

- The effectiveness of the e3 model hinges on the follow-up discipleship of new believers. Nationals do not feel equipped well enough to disciple all of the new believers following the campaign.

- e3 Partners must work hard to ensure that dependency issues do not arise.

- e3 Partners should trust its national leadership when it comes to choosing where and with whom to work.

Appendix 3
The 7 Basic Commands of Jesus
* adapted with permission from George Patterson

Jesus taught many things during His time on earth. The Apostle John says that if all of Jesus' teachings were recorded that the world itself could not contain all the books (John 21:25). So how then do we as leaders obey Jesus' command to "teach everything that I have commanded"? (Matthew 28:18-20) Although that seems like an impossible task, all of Jesus' commands fit into one of seven categories that we call "The Basic Commands of Jesus".

Train your disciples to *memorize, apply and reproduce* these **7 Basic Commands**. Discuss the importance of the commands, and work through the Scriptures together. You can reinforce this teaching by showing how any of Jesus' commands recorded in Scripture would fall into one of these categories. The most effective use is to MODEL the Basic Commands for them, ASSIST them with memorization and application, WATCH them teach it to others, then LEAVE them to reproduce.

How do we teach people to obey all that Jesus has commanded? Dr. George Patterson developed the "7 Basic Commands of Jesus" as a tool to communicate with semi-literate and illiterate people during his decades of missionary service in Honduras. While the list is by no means exhaustive, it does indeed cover the primary teaching emphases of our LORD.

1. **Repent, believe and receive the Holy Spirit**

   Mark 1:15 "The time has come," he said. "The kingdom of God is near. Repent and believe the good news!"

2. **Be baptized**

   Matthew 28:19 "Therefore go and make disciples of all nations, baptizing them in the name of the Father and of the Son and of the Holy Spirit,"

3. **Break bread in Communion and worship**

   Matthew 26:26-28 "While they were eating, Jesus took bread, gave thanks and broke it, and gave it to his disciples, saying, 'Take and eat; this is my body.' Then he took the cup, gave thanks and offered it to them, saying, 'Drink from it, all of you. This is my blood of the covenant, which is poured out for many for the forgiveness of sins'"

4. **Love God and fellow man**

   Mark 12:30-31 "Love the Lord your God with all your heart and with all your soul and with all your mind and with all your strength. The second is this: 'Love your neighbor as yourself.' There is no commandment greater than these"

5. **Pray in all things**

   Matthew 6:9 "This, then, is how you should pray: Our Father in heaven, hallowed be your name, your kingdom come, your will be done on earth as it is in heaven. Give us today our daily bread. Forgive us our debts, as we also have forgiven our debtors. And lead us not into temptation, but deliver us from the evil one."

6. **Give generously (time, talents, treasure)**

   Luke 6:38 "Give, and it will be given to you. A good measure, pressed down, shaken together and running over, will be poured into your lap. For with the measure you use, it will be measured to you."

7. **Make disciples**

   Matthew 28:18-20 "Then Jesus came to them and said, All authority in heaven and on earth has been given to me. Therefore go and make disciples of all nations, baptizing them in the name of the Father and of the Son and of the Holy Spirit, and teaching them to obey everything I have commanded you. And surely I am with you always, to the very end of the age."

In John 14:15, Jesus said, "If you love me, you will obey what I command."

Teaching the 7 Basic Commands of Jesus using the parable from Matthew 7:24-27:

Jesus said, "Therefore <u>everyone who hears these words of mine and puts them into practice is like a wise man who built his house on the rock</u>. The rain came down, the streams rose, and the winds blew and beat against that house; yet it did not fall, because it had its foundation on the rock. But everyone who hears these words of mine and does not put them into practice is like a foolish man who built his house on sand. The rain came down, the streams rose, and the winds blew and beat against that house, and it fell with a great crash."

7 Basic Commands of Jesus

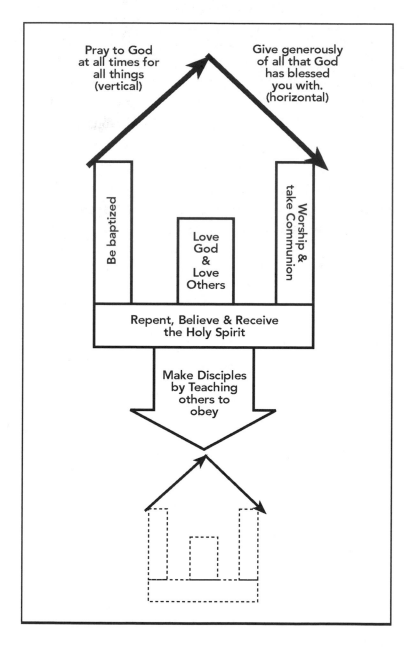

Pray to God at all times for all things (vertical)

Give generously of all that God has blessed you with. (horizontal)

Be baptized

Love God & Love Others

Worship & take Communion

Repent, Believe & Receive the Holy Spirit

Make Disciples by Teaching others to obey

Notes

Chapter 1

[1] David Garrison, Church Planting Movements: How God is Redeeming a Lost World (Midlothian, VA: WIGTake Resources, 2004), 21.

[2] See <http://www.ggrobinson.com> for a free download of the dissertation entitled, "The Ministry of E3 Partners as a Case Study of Strategic Cross-cultural Short-term Missions"

[3] See <http://www.e3mission.org> for a list of current opportunities.

Chapter 2

[4] I use the term "majority world" throughout this book in reference to those nations that are not a part of the historic West. In the past many of these areas were referred to as the "Third World" or as "developing nations", but these latter terms are dated and somewhat condescending.

[5] With regard to the supernatural gifts of the Spirit, I consider myself to be a "cautious continualist," meaning that I believe God does continue to do miracles today: however I am careful to make sure that any such claims are in accordance with and not contrary to Biblical revelation. I'm extremely optimistic that God can and does intervene in the daily affairs of men in such a way that Jesus Christ will be exalted through the Gospel.

[6] See Ralph Winter, "The Greatest Danger . . . The Re-Amateurization of Mission," Missions Frontier Bulletin, March-April, 1996.

[7] David Filbeck, Yes, God of the Gentiles, Too: The Missionary Message of the Old Testament (Wheaton, IL: Billy Graham Center, 1994), 11.

[8] Roger Peterson, Gordon Aeshliman and R. Wayne Sneed, Maximum Impact Short-Term Mission (Minneapolis: STEMPress, 2003), 199-207.

[9] Bryan A. Slater, "Short-term Missions: Biblical Considerations," EMQ Online October, 2000. 1. < http://www.emqonline.com >, last accessed January 10, 2007.

[10] Ibid.

[11] Randall Gary Friesen, "Improving the Long-term Impact of Short-term Missions" (based on his doctoral thesis, University of South Africa), 2004. 1.

[12] John Piper, "Let the Nations Be Glad," Grand Rapids, Baker Books, 1993, 15.

13 John Miles, "An Assessment of STM," (M.A. Dissertation, Birmingham Bible Institute, 2000), 12.

[14] A. Wayne Meece, "Was Paul a Short-term Missionary?" The Gospel Unhindered, edited by Doug Priest, Jr. (Pasadena: William Carey Library, 1994), 216-217.

[15] Roland Allen, Missionary Methods: St. Paul's or Ours? (Grand Rapids: Eerdman's, 1998), 10 ff.

[16] Miles, 2000, 12.

[17] Slater, 2000, 3.

[18] J. Herbert Kane, A Concise History of the Christian World Mission (Grand Rapids: Baker Books, 1978), 9.

19 Donald Kitchen, "The Impact and Effectiveness of Short-term Missionaries" (Ph.D. dissertation, Dallas, TX: Dallas Theological Seminary Department of World Missions, 1976), 24.

20 Meece, 1994, 216.

21 Michael Green, Thirty Years that Changed the World: The Book of Acts for Today (Grand Rapids: Eerdmans Publishing, 2004), 48.

22 Ibid.

23 Slater, 2000, 3.

24 Miles, 2000, 12. Miles notes that Philip arrived in Caesarea in Acts 8:40 and is still there in Acts 21:8. The span of time between those two citations is estimated to be around 20 years; however, no proof can be made that Philip resided and ministered in that context for the whole of that time.

25 Green, 2004, 135.

26 Peterson et al, 198.

Chapter 3

27 Guthrie, 109.

28 John Mark Terry, "The History of Missions in the Early Church," Missiology, edited by Terry, Smith and Anderson (Nashville, TN: Broadman and Holman, 1998), 167-8.

29 Peterson et al., 255.

30 Terry, 171.

31 Ibid.,171 and 176-177.

32 Ibid., 172 and 179-180.

33 George G. Hunter, III, The Celtic Way of Evangelism (Nashville, TN: Abingdon, 2000), 26.

34 Ibid., 77.

35 Miles, 2000, 12.

36 Sam Wellman, William Carey: Father of Modern Missions (Uhrichsville, OH: Barbour Publishing, 1997), 201-202.

37 Baar, 2.

38 The word "modern" here refers not to contemporary times, but to the era following the Middle Ages where Western technological advancements took place rapidly. This missiological paradigm shift that seems to have occurred in Carey's time would have taken place during what historians refer to as the Age of Enlightenment.
< http://en.wikipedia.org/wiki/Modern_history> January 29, 2007.

39 Justice Anderson, "The Great Century and Beyond," Missiology, edited by Terry, Smith and Anderson (Nashville, TN: Broadman and Holman, 1998), 204.

40 Ibid., 217.

41 Ralph D. Winter, "Four Men, Three Eras, Two Transitions: Modern Missions," Perspectives on the World Christian Movement, edited by Ralph D. Winter and Steven Hawthorne (Pasadena, CA: William Carey Library, 1999), 258.

42 Daniel Yergin, Richard Vietor and Peter Evans, "Fettered Flight: Globalization and the Airline Industry," Cambridge Energy Research Associates, Inc.(2000):17-18.
< http://www.air-transport.org/econ/files/FetteredFlight.pdf >

43 U.S. Federal Aviation Administration. <
http://api.hq.faa.gov/forecast05/Table7.PDF > March 2, 2005.

44 Wesley Paddock, "Are Short-Termers the Future of Missions?" Christian Standard, 127:30. July 26, 1992, 630-631.

45 Susan G. Loobie, "Short-term Missions: Is It Worth It?" Latin America Mission News Service, January, 2000.

46 Peterson et al., 253.
47 Tim Gibson, Steve Hawthorne, Richard Krekel and Kn Moy, editors, Stepping Out – A Guide to Short-term Missions (Seattle, WA: YWAM Publishing, 1992), 5.
48 Friesen, 2004, 2.

Chapter 4

49 Gailyn Van Rheenan, Biblical Foundations and Contemporary Strategies: Missions (Grand Rapids, MI: Zondervan, 1996), 20.
50 See the article by John R.W. Stott that expounds on this thought. <http://www.uscwm.org/mobilization_division/resources/perspectives_reader_pdf's/A01_Stott_TheLivingGod.pdf>
51 Carrie Baar, "Short-term Student Missions and the Needs of Nationals" (M.A. Thesis, Denver Seminary, 2003), 19.
52 < http://www.wycliffe.org/go/home.asp?type=vacancy > This site shows more than 50 opportunities ranging from bible translator, to MK teacher, to database administrator, to truck driver. Last accessed June 30, 2006.
53 Miles, 29.
54 See <http://www.shorttermmissions.com>.
55 Peterson et al., 27.
56 J. Herbert Kane, Wanted: World Christians (Grand Rapids, MI: Baker Book House, 1986), 208-209.
57 Peterson et al.,198.
58 Filbeck, 65.
59 For more on this topic see Michael Pocock,. "Gaining Long-Term Mileage from Short-Term Programs," Evangelical Missions Quarterly, v. 23 no. 2 (April, 1987): 154-160.
60 Bob Roberts, Jr.. Glocalization (Grand Rapids: Zondervan Publishing, 2007). See also < http://glocal.net >.
61 < http://www.thepeaceplan.com > January 10, 2007. The acronym is based upon what Warren feels would answer many of the world's greatest ills: Plant Churches, Equip Servant Leaders, Assist the Poor, Care for the Sick, and Educate the Next Generation.
62 Winter, 1996, 5.
63 Erwin McManus is the Lead Pastor of Mosaic Church in Los Angeles, CA. That church has a legacy of missions-mindedness that predates his involvement, but has continued to flourish and expand since his arrival.
64 Friesen, 1.
65 Peterson et al.,18.
66 Jim Montgomery, DAWN 2000: 7 Million Churches to Go (Pasadena, CA: William Carey Library, 1989), 38-39.
67 Greg Livingstone, Planting Churches in Muslim Cities: A Team Approach (Grand Rapids, MI: Baker Books, 1993), 73.

Chapter 5

68 Peterson et al.,153. This figure does not appear in the text, but I have created it because I feel it communicates the necessary balance of STM more accurately.
69 These are the terms given by the authors in an attempt to standardize the vocabulary of STM, as well as to make participants more aware of the various aspects of each others' roles. "Goer-guest" corresponds to the person going cross-cultural on an STM. "Sender" refers to the entity through which the trip is

arranged (local church, mission agency, or STM organization). "Recipient-host" is the designation given to the nationals who are receiving the team.
[70] Ibid., 174.

Chapter 6

[71] Tom Steffen, Passing the Baton: Church Planting that Empowers (La Habra: Center for Organizational & Ministry Development, 1993), 170.
[72] Garrison, 2004, 262-266.
[73] Read Luke 10:2-20 for a description of the instructions that Jesus gave to his disciples when he sent them out.
[74] Most of the church planting coaches working within an e3 national strategy are bi-vocational. By "providing resources" we mean that we sometimes cover travel expenses and provide tools such as the Evangecube and First Steps manuals to aid in equipping and mobilizing for church planting.

Chapter 7

[75] George Patterson and Richard Scoggins, Church Multiplication Guide: The Miracle of Church Reproduction (Pasadena, CA: William Carey Library, 2002), 12.
[76] Andy Stanley, Visioneering. Multnomah Publishers: Sisters, OR, 1999. 17.
[77] Charles Brock, Indigenous Church Planting (Neosho, Missouri: Church Growth International, 1994), 98.
[78] Patterson and Scoggins, 84.
[79] Garrison, 2004, 175.
[80] Ibid., 177.
[81] Charles & Win Arn, The Master's Plan for Making Disciples (Grand Rapids: Baker Books, 1982), 29.
[82] Meece, 1994, 210.
[83] R. Bruce Carlton, Acts 29: Practical Training in Facilitating CPMs Among the Neglected Harvest Fields (Bangalore: Radical Obedience Publishing, 2003), 21.
[84] Carlton, 21.
[85] Garrison, 2004, 181.

Chapter 8

[86] David Garrison, Church Planting Movements, Richmond, VA: International Mission Board, 2000.
[87] Miles, 23.
[88] I prefer to use George Patterson's "Basic Commands of Jesus" here because it provides a crucial, yet easily transferable understanding of what it means to be a follower of Jesus. You can learn more about this in Appendix 3 and by going to <http://www.mentorandmultiply.com>.
[89] We don't model the forms so as not to export non-biblical Western traditions. Rather, we emphasize those elements of church that are explicit in Scripture.
[90] These "signal systems" are described at length in Dr. Donald K. Smith's crucial book on Christian communication called Creating Understanding: A Handbook for Christian Communication Across Cultural Landscapes, Zondervan, 1992.
[91] In some areas of the world where partnering with a mother church is either not possible or could cause problems, e3 Partners adapts this typical model and works with indigenous evangelists and church planters. The core elements of partnering in prayer, evangelism and discipleship in a collaborative effort to plant new reproducing churches remains constant even on these adapted campaigns.
[92] Garrison, 2004, 344.

Chapter 9

[93] For the purposes of this book I have attempted to present complicated research in layman's terms. If you want to read the technical academic presentation you can download the full dissertation at <http://www.ggrobinson.com>.

[94] This longitudinal approach spanned on average a three month time period.

[95] Statistical significance in this study was defined as having >/= .95 chance that there is a relationship between the independent variable (either the LDC or the presence of the STM team) and the dependent variable (a change in the attitude toward or frequency of implementation of the noted church planting principle).

[96] A complete summary of the findings from my qualitative research can be found in Appendix Two.

[97] The First Steps CP manual that serves as one of the primary tools in these partnerships clarifies that the "mother church model" (where an existing church plants a new church and takes responsibility for helping it to reach spiritual maturity) is the most effective means to seeing churches become established and healthy. See First Steps: Mobilizing Your Church into God's Harvest Fields, Plano, TX: e3 Partners Ministries, 2005, 88-9.

[98] This tract has a section at the end where personal information is requested including name, address and contact information. A copy can be found in the chapter entitled "Evangelize" in the First Steps manual.

[99] Quoted from a personal conversation with Mike Jorgensen dated February 2007.

[100] The "Omega Course" was developed and published by the Alliance for Saturation Church Planting. This curriculum is extensive but very practical, helping leaders develop and implement plans for establishing reproducing churches by the time of completion.

[101] Some might question why e3 Partners has not taken more care to study church planting retention in the past. Until the reorganization from GMF to e3 Partners there were no national leaders receiving any type of on-going financial assistance from the organization. Leaders that organized and hosted STM campaigns were given a love offering at the end of the campaign. Without on-going support most of these national leaders could not afford to travel around their country and check on the status of their work. The e3 Partnership Program was established in part to help create an on-going revenue pool for NDs so that they could be employed "full-time" by the organization and could then be expected to gather this much-needed information. The move was not retroactive however because it would be next to impossible to travel in some cases to hundreds of locations to check on the status of churches planted in years gone by. Instead, e3 Partners requires its national directors to keep records and status of all newly established works from the point of their joining staff full-time.

Chapter 10

[102] <http://en.wikipedia.org/wiki/Serendipity>

[103] In working to trace the historical and missiological development of e3 Partners I conducted an in-depth interview with the current CEO, Curtis Hail. Hail's keen insight and long history with the organization have proven invaluable to my research. Rather than conduct an oral interview where much would be lost in the asking and telling, I wrote out a list of questions that Hail thought through at length and then responded in detail. Unless otherwise noted, much of the information in this chapter has been gleaned from Hail's responses.

[104] Peter Drucker, Innovation and Entrepreneurship (New York: Harper Collins Publishing, 1985), 37.

[105] The concept behind this idea was really nothing new. Church Growth specialists had long heralded the axiom "New units grow; old units don't." Downey had himself been steeped in this concept as a SBC pastor in directing his own Sunday School ministry as new classes grew more rapidly than older established ones that had plateaued. So Downey was quick to recognize how this principle applied in his experiences in Mexico and capitalized upon it to help plant new reproducing churches.

[106] Baptist ecclesiology has sometimes been ambiguous as to what constitutes a "church." The Mexican Baptist Convention opted to call these new work sites "mission points" or "mission churches" until there was a certain number of baptized believers and an ordained pastor. This approach has become firmly entrenched in many areas as the result of the early missiological blind spots among LTMs. Downey, however recognized the legitimacy of the small group (meta-church, cell church, house church) as the basic building block for a new church. Once again, GMF found itself riding the front end of a missiological wave substantiated by many denominations and mission agencies around the world.

[107] Hail, 2006.

[108] Ibid.

[109] Ibid.

[110] See <http://www.simplysharejesus.com>.

[111] The introduction of GLN brought an upsurge of emphasis within the organization focused on equipping nationals. In keeping with the simplicity-based success of the Evangecube, I, along with Mike Jorgensen and Sam Ingrassia started to compile, collaborate and refine CP training materials that were easy to understand. The outcome of that effort is "First Steps: Mobilizing Your Church to Multiply Your Church," a curriculum that has been translated into over a dozen languages and is being used as the ground-level training of every national we work with. Our goal was to make CP as easy to understand as the Evangecube. This resource is available at <http://www.evangecube.org/dresources.html>, Accessed February 14, 2007.

[112] Hail, 2006.

[113] Garrison, 2000, 33-36.

[114] Hail, 2006.

[115] Ibid.

[116] e3 Partners is not so presumptuous to think that we are the only ones "doing it right." There are many mission organizations that are working to use STM as a part of their long-term strategy.

[117] In the quantitative portion of my doctoral research I used several national-only campaigns as my control group with which to compare those campaigns that featured North American STM teams. There are several national e3 leaders that are now coordinating more national-only campaigns each year than North American ones.

[118] Sam Ingrassia, "The Ministry of e3 Partners" (speech presented at the annual meeting of e3 Partners Ministries, Plano, Texas, January 2006).

[119] Hail, 2006.

[120] These advertisements feature photographs of various individuals from different ethnic groups around the world and the subject's name is placed in the blank to drive the point home.

Chapter 11

[121] David Hesselgrave, Planting Churches Cross-Culturally (Grand Rapids: Baker Book House, 1980), 20.

[122] This figure is only inclusive of first generation trainees. Most of these trainers commit to reproduce the training they received by equipping all of the members of their church. Some of them go on to become trainers working alongside their e3 national directors as part of the national strategy. Therefore, this number displays the tip of the iceberg with regard to the tens of thousands that have been trained in second or third generation LDCs, most of which go unreported.

[123] This figure was reported by Mike Jorgensen and is based upon all national trainers' reports for both Evangecube Training Seminars and First Steps LDCs.

[124] Some missiologists may think that the measurement of POFs is less valid than baptisms. Our reason for measuring the one over the other is both theological and ecclesiological in nature. Baptism is an ordinance of the local church. Because e3 Partners is not a denomination or a church, we submit to the authority of the local churches being established to conduct and track the baptisms of those making POFs.

[125] It is a matter of unwritten policy that numbers evangelized and POFs from large group gatherings are not counted in e3 Partners totals. The ministry does not typically engage in mass campaigns where a single evangelist is preaching to large crowds because such a format does not empower and mobilize the laity. This is not a critique of the crusade approach, but rather a distinctive of the ministry.

[126] David J. Barrett and Todd M. Johnson show in World Christian Trends AD 30 – AD 2200 that the number of "evangelism hours" inputted by what they call "part-timers" outnumbers (70 million vs. 5.5 million hours) that of "full-timers," "macroevangelists," "mega-evangelists," and "global evangelists" combined. (687)

[127] Follow-up studies have been conducted in one of the three countries that participated in my research. The national director for the country of Bolivia helped e3 Partners conduct an informal study of areas where churches were started on STM campaigns in 2005. Of 27 areas where new church starts were attempted, 22 of those were still gathering for worship over one year later. That means 81% of the churches remain. That statistic in itself is not at all discouraging; however, when the full follow-up report was completed we learned that six additional churches have been planted by those groups with no assistance from our STM teams. Therefore, the net success rate for establishing churches in this area of Bolivia is over 100%!

Chapter 12
[128] Garrison, 2004, 188-189.
[129] Ibid. 249.